Communications in Computer and Information Science

2872

Series Editors

Gang Li, *School of Information Technology, Deakin University, Burwood, VIC, Australia*

Joaquim Filipe, *Polytechnic Institute of Setúbal, Setúbal, Portugal*

Zhiwei Xu, *Chinese Academy of Sciences, Beijing, China*

Rationale
The CCIS series is devoted to the publication of proceedings of computer science conferences. Its aim is to efficiently disseminate original research results in informatics in printed and electronic form. While the focus is on publication of peer-reviewed full papers presenting mature work, inclusion of reviewed short papers reporting on work in progress is welcome, too. Besides globally relevant meetings with internationally representative program committees guaranteeing a strict peer-reviewing and paper selection process, conferences run by societies or of high regional or national relevance are also considered for publication.

Topics
The topical scope of CCIS spans the entire spectrum of informatics ranging from foundational topics in the theory of computing to information and communications science and technology and a broad variety of interdisciplinary application fields.

Information for Volume Editors and Authors
Publication in CCIS is free of charge. No royalties are paid, however, we offer registered conference participants temporary free access to the online version of the conference proceedings on SpringerLink (http://link.springer.com) by means of an http referrer from the conference website and/or a number of complimentary printed copies, as specified in the official acceptance email of the event.

CCIS proceedings can be published in time for distribution at conferences or as post-proceedings, and delivered in the form of printed books and/or electronically as USBs and/or e-content licenses for accessing proceedings at SpringerLink. Furthermore, CCIS proceedings are included in the CCIS electronic book series hosted in the SpringerLink digital library at http://link.springer.com/bookseries/7899. Conferences publishing in CCIS are allowed to use Online Conference Service (OCS) for managing the whole proceedings lifecycle (from submission and reviewing to preparing for publication) free of charge.

Publication process
The language of publication is exclusively English. Authors publishing in CCIS have to sign the Springer CCIS copyright transfer form, however, they are free to use their material published in CCIS for substantially changed, more elaborate subsequent publications elsewhere. For the preparation of the camera-ready papers/files, authors have to strictly adhere to the Springer CCIS Authors' Instructions and are strongly encouraged to use the CCIS LaTeX style files or templates.

Abstracting/Indexing
CCIS is abstracted/indexed in DBLP, Google Scholar, EI-Compendex, Mathematical Reviews, SCImago, Scopus. CCIS volumes are also submitted for the inclusion in ISI Proceedings.

How to start
To start the evaluation of your proposal for inclusion in the CCIS series, please send an e-mail to ccis@springer.com

Shaukat Ali · Francisco Chicano ·
Alberto Moraglio

Editors

Quantum Computing and Artificial Intelligence

Second International Workshop, QC+AI 2026
Singapore, January 27, 2026
Proceedings

 Springer

Editors
Shaukat Ali
Simula Research Laboratory
Oslo, Norway

Francisco Chicano
ITIS Software, University of Malaga
Málaga, Spain

Alberto Moraglio
University of Exeter
London, UK

ISSN 1865-0929 ISSN 1865-0937 (electronic)
Communications in Computer and Information Science
ISBN 978-3-032-17624-0 ISBN 978-3-032-17625-7 (eBook)
https://doi.org/10.1007/978-3-032-17625-7

This Springer imprint is published by the registered company Springer Nature Switzerland AG
The registered company address is: Gewerbestrasse 11, 6330 Cham, Switzerland

If disposing of this product, please recycle the paper.

Preface

Quantum computers, albeit on a small scale, are becoming increasingly accessible to the public, for example, through companies like IBM, Google, and D-Wave. Naturally, this calls for leveraging quantum computers to enhance classical Artificial Intelligence (AI), for example, to improve predictive performance or enable faster training by exploiting quantum mechanical principles such as superposition and entanglement. To this end, there is a growing interest in quantum artificial intelligence (QAI) to exploit quantum computing (QC) to enhance classical AI techniques. On the other hand, there is also an increasing interest in applying classical AI techniques to solve QC problems (AI4QC), such as in quantum software engineering, quantum circuit design, and quantum optimization approaches.

The Second International Workshop on Quantum Computing and Artificial Intelligence (QC+AI 2026) was held in conjunction with the 40th Annual AAAI Conference on Artificial Intelligence (AAAI 2026) in Singapore, on January 27, 2026. The workshop sought contributions encompassing theoretical and applied advances in QAI, as well as contributions that apply classical AI techniques to various aspects of QC, including optimization problems arising in the QC context. The workshop received 17 submissions, which were peer-reviewed by at least three reviewers in a single-blind process. A total of 3 lightning talks and 7 full papers were accepted for presentation at the workshop. We include in this volume the accepted full papers, which focus on quantum optimization and quantum machine learning.

We thank our invited keynote speaker, Jayne Thompson from Nanyang Technological University, for accepting the invitation to participate in this workshop. Jayne showed that executing complex strategies carries a fundamental energetic cost for classical agents and explained how quantum agents can overcome these limits, making decisions with less memory and energy.

We also thank the AAAI organization for their support in organizing this workshop, the authors who submitted to QC+AI 2026, and the program committee members for their hard work during the reviewing process.

December 2025

Shaukat Ali
Francisco Chicano
Alberto Moraglio

Organization

Program Committee Chairs

Shaukat Ali   Simula Research Laboratory, Norway
Francisco Chicano   ITIS Software, University of Malaga, Spain
Alberto Moraglio   University of Exeter, UK

Program Committee

Paolo Arcaini	National Institute of Informatics, Japan
Eric Bourreau	LIRMM, France
Samuel Yen-Chi Chen	Wells Fargo, USA
Philippe Codognet	JFLI - CNRS/Sorbonne University, France/University of Tokyo, Japan
Zakaria Abdelmoiz Dahi	INRIA Lille, France
Bilel Derbel	CRIStAL (University of Lille), France
Sebastian Feld	Delft University of Technology, Netherlands
Mikel Garcia de Andoin	TECNALIA & University of the Basque Country UPV/EHU, Spain
Joongheon Kim	Korea University, South Korea
Shiho Kim	Yonsei University, South Korea
KC Kong	University of Kansas, USA
Junyong Lee	Yonsei University, South Korea
Gabriel Luque	University of Málaga, Spain
Eñaut Mendiluze Usandizaga	Simula Research Laboratory, Norway
Shunya Minami	National Institute of Advanced Industrial Science and Technology, Japan
Eneko Osaba	TECNALIA Research & Innovation, Spain
Matthieu Parizy	Fujitsu Ltd., Japan
Jihong Park	Singapore University of Technology and Design, Singapore
Dheeraj Peddireddy	Purdue University, USA
Shinobu Saito	NTT Corporation, Japan
Aritra Sarkar	Delft University of Technology, Netherlands
Ruhan Wang	Indiana University, USA

Saving Resources with Quantum Agents

Jayne Thompson

Nanyang Technological University, Singapore

Abstract. Autonomous vehicles navigating busy streets, an algorithmic trader seeking to maximize returns—all represent autonomous agents. Each executes complex strategies—continually adapting their actions based on past experiences. As society pushes such agentic intelligence to perform ever more complex tasks, the computational resource requirements of such agents is growing in tandem—contributing to chip shortages, and a growing energy footprint of such technologies. Indeed with the rapid advances in large language models, the memory resources costs and energetic costs required are growing in tandem at unsustainable rates. Is this merely a result of engineering inefficiency or is there a fundamental energetic cost to executing complex strategies? Here we demonstrate that there is a fundamental energetic cost in executing a target strategy—one that all classical agents must obey. We illustrate that cost is unavoidable, born from the need for an agent to be prepared for any possible future contingency. We show how quantum computing can surpass such bounds. The end result is a quantum agent that is equally prepared for future contingencies, while using fundamentally less memory and energy. Thus the most efficient way to make decisions in the face of future uncertainty is quantum mechanical.

Contents

QUBO-Based Subset Selection for Efficient Fine-Tuning of Vision–Language Models

Akihiro Yoshida[1(✉)] ⓘ, Keiichiro Yamamura[1] ⓘ, Hiroki Ishikura[1] ⓘ,
Shinjiro Hirai[2], Ken Kawano[2], Yoshihiko Fujisawa[2], and Katsuki Fujisawa[1] ⓘ

[1] Institute of Integrated Research, Institute of Science Tokyo, 4259, Nagatsuda-cho,
Midori-ku, Yokohama, Kanagawa 2268501, Japan
`{yoshida.a.aad4,yamamura.k.d731,ishikura.h.de21,`
`fujisawa.k.2110}@m.isct.ac.jp`
[2] Mathematical and Computing Science, School of Science, Institute of Science
Tokyo, 2-12-1, Ookayama, Meguro-ku, Tokyo 152-8550, Japan
`{hirai.s.e86c,kawano.k.4e8f,fujisawa.y.5bdc}@m.isct.ac.jp`

Abstract. Fine-tuning large-scale Vision–Language Models (VLMs) is computationally demanding, motivating the need for efficient data utilization. Existing subset selection methods, such as COINCIDE, primarily focus on distribution matching but overlook instance-level utility, redundancy, and task-specific reasoning relevance. We propose QUBO-based Informative Subset Selection (QUBISS), a unified framework that formulates data selection as a Quadratic Unconstrained Binary Optimization (QUBO) problem. QUBISS jointly maximizes task-relevant data utility and minimizes sample redundancy to promote diversity and compactness. Central to our method is the task vector, which quantifies the semantic contribution of textual information to reasoning performance and integrates it into the QUBO utility term. When applied to fine-tuning LLaVA v1.5, QUBISS selects only 20% of a 665K image–text dataset while achieving results superior or comparable to COINCIDE on both cognition-oriented (MME-C) and perception-oriented (MME-P) benchmarks. The observed gains underscore the value of task-aware semantic guidance for cost-efficient multimodal fine-tuning. Furthermore, advances in large-scale quantum solvers could further enhance QUBISS by directly solving large QUBOs without decomposing them into cluster-level subproblems, thereby mitigating suboptimality arising from problem partitioning.

Keywords: Vision language model · Quadratic unconstrained binary optimization problem (QUBO) · Subset selection

1 Introduction

Vision–Language Models (VLMs) represent a major breakthrough in artificial intelligence, unifying visual and textual understanding by combining the strengths of computer vision and natural language processing. These multimodal

© The Author(s), under exclusive license to Springer Nature Switzerland AG 2026
S. Ali et al. (Eds.): QC+AI 2026, CCIS 2872, pp. 1–17, 2026.
https://doi.org/10.1007/978-3-032-17625-7_1

models underpin a wide range of emerging applications, such as zero-shot visual question answering, object localization, and zero-shot segmentation. However, achieving state-of-the-art performance typically requires fine-tuning these large models on task-specific data, which is computationally expensive and resource-intensive. This challenge is further amplified by the scaling law phenomenon—originally established for LLMs—which states that model performance scales predictably with model size, dataset size, and computational resources. Similar trends have also been observed in VLMs [21], making the cost of fine-tuning particularly prohibitive.

A natural response to the high fine-tuning cost is data subset selection—fine-tuning on a strategically chosen fraction of the training data. Prior studies, such as COINCIDE [11] and TAROT [4], primarily focus on distribution matching, aiming to select samples so that the subset statistically resembles the full dataset. However, this line of work often overlooks two critical factors that directly impact fine-tuning efficiency: data utility, which measures how informative each instance is for the target task, and redundancy, which quantifies how replaceable an instance is by others in the subset. Moreover, recent findings highlight that caption specificity—the presence of fine-grained details in textual descriptions—plays a key role in downstream performance [7]. Yet existing subset selection methods seldom consider such semantic specificity when estimating sample utility, limiting their ability to capture reasoning-relevant information.

To address these limitations, we propose QUBO-based Informative Subset Selection (QUBISS), a novel framework that unifies task-aware representation modeling with QUBO-based combinatorial optimization for efficient data selection. QUBISS formulates the subset selection problem as a Quadratic Unconstrained Binary Optimization (QUBO) task, enabling a single objective that jointly captures data utility and redundancy. A key innovation of QUBISS is the introduction of a task vector without training an auxiliary network, which quantifies the semantic contribution of fine-grained textual details—crucial for reasoning-oriented tasks. For each image–text pair, we compute embeddings of (i) the original conversation and (ii) a de-specified variant in which salient details are replaced by generic placeholders. The difference between these embeddings defines the task vector, emphasizing reasoning-relevant information that would otherwise be lost in de-specified conversations. This task vector is integrated into the QUBO utility term, biasing the selection toward samples that preserve detailed and semantically rich conversations. At the same time, the redundancy term penalizes mutual similarity, ensuring diversity and compactness within the selected subset. By seamlessly integrating task-sensitive semantic guidance with QUBO-based optimization, QUBISS provides the first unified formulation that simultaneously achieves reasoning-oriented data utility maximization and redundancy control.

We evaluate QUBISS using the LLaVA v1.5 [14] to assess its effectiveness in large-scale multimodal fine-tuning. In our experiments, we applied QUBISS to a dataset of 665K image–text pairs and extracted a 20% informative subset for fine-tuning. Despite using only a fraction of the data, QUBISS achieved performance comparable to or superior to the COINCIDE baseline on both MME-C (cognition-oriented) and MME-P (perception-oriented) benchmarks. The improvement in MME-C, in particular, demonstrates the effectiveness of the task vector, which guides the selection toward samples rich in fine-grained and reasoning-relevant details. These results highlight that incorporating task-sensitive semantics into the subset selection process can substantially reduce fine-tuning costs while preserving reasoning performance.

2   Related Work

Fine-tuning deep learning models, particularly large-scale ones, incurs substantial computational costs. To alleviate this, dataset selection has been explored as a means of improving computational efficiency while maintaining performance [5,10]. This line of research aims to identify informative subsets that preserve task performance at a fraction of the training cost. A similar motivation underlies efforts in large language models (LLMs), where the data used during pretraining and fine-tuning critically influence adaptation and generalization [22,27]. For example, LIMA [27] demonstrates that 1,000 high-quality samples can outperform large-scale uncurated data, while D4 [22] removes duplicated instances via cluster-wise filtering. Recently, linear programming has been utilized for dataset selection [26]. TagCos [25] leverages gradient information to select data subsets, but it incurs considerable computational costs due to the need to compute gradients for all instances. These works highlight the potential of data selection to yield efficient yet high-performing models.

Recent studies have also observed scaling-law-like behavior in Vision–Language Models (VLMs) [20], suggesting that careful subset selection can achieve competitive performance with reduced data budgets for VLMs. COINCIDE [11] employs a smaller VLM as a feature extractor, mapping samples into a latent space for clustering-based selection that preserves the overall data distribution. TAROT [4] utilizes optimal transport to extract representative subsets that align with the source data distribution. However, such approaches mainly focus on preserving distributional coverage, potentially overlooking redundancy among selected samples. Recent work has attempted to estimate sample utility via influence functions [24] or instance-wise cost models [1], but these methods require significant additional computation, such as training auxiliary networks. More recently, dataset selection for specific domains has emerged, such as Proctag [19], which targets document dataset selection via OCR and layout detection.

Despite recent progress, existing VLM dataset selection methods rarely integrate both data utility and redundancy control without training auxiliary networks or performing backpropagation. Our study addresses this gap by formulating the problem as a Quadratic Unconstrained Binary Optimization (QUBO) problem, enabling explicit modeling of these two objectives within a single formulation. Furthermore, we introduce a task vector to capture reasoning-relevant textual information, guiding the selection toward samples that enhance reasoning-intensive capabilities. This combination distinguishes our approach from prior clustering- or distance-based methods.

3   Preliminaries

This section introduces the fundamental concepts of Vision–Language Models (VLMs) in Sect. 3.1 and the formulation of QUBO in Sect. 3.2.

3.1   Vision–Language Models

Vision–Language Models (VLMs) are multimodal architectures that jointly process visual and textual inputs by aligning them within a shared embedding space. A representative example is LLaVA [14], which combines a pretrained Vision Transformer as the image encoder with a large language model—Vicuna [2], a fine-tuned variant of Llama 2 [23]—as the text decoder. During training, image–text pairs are used to align their latent representations, enabling cross-modal reasoning and understanding.

This shared embedding facilitates a broad range of multimodal tasks, including:

- Visual question answering: generating textual answers to questions about images.
- Image captioning: producing natural-language descriptions of visual scenes.
- Text-to-image generation: synthesizing images from textual prompts.
- Zero-shot reasoning: performing unseen tasks such as object localization or semantic segmentation without task-specific supervision.

By bridging visual perception with linguistic reasoning, VLMs exhibit human-like generalization and serve as powerful backbones for multimodal understanding and reasoning. Fine-tuning typically employs a next-token prediction objective over instruction–image pairs, adapting the model to specific downstream domains or tasks.

3.2   Quadratic Unconstrained Binary Optimization (QUBO)

A Quadratic Unconstrained Binary Optimization (QUBO) problem seeks to maximize a quadratic objective over binary decision variables, formally defined as:

$$\max_{\boldsymbol{x}\in\{0,1\}^n} \boldsymbol{x}^\top Q \boldsymbol{x}, \tag{1}$$

where:

- $\boldsymbol{x} = (x_1, x_2, \ldots, x_n)^\top$ is a vector of n binary decision variables.
- $Q \in \mathbb{R}^{n \times n}$ is a symmetric coefficient matrix, referred to as the QUBO matrix, whose entries $Q_{i,j}$ encode the contribution and pairwise interactions between variables.

Expanding the objective yields:

$$\boldsymbol{x}^\top Q \boldsymbol{x} = \sum_{i=1}^{n} Q_{i,i} x_i + \sum_{i<j} 2 Q_{i,j} x_i x_j. \tag{2}$$

The first term, $Q_{i,i}x_i$, represents the individual utility (or cost) of selecting item i (i.e., when $x_i = 1$), while the second term, $2Q_{i,j}x_ix_j$, captures the interaction effect between items i and j, which becomes active only when both variables are selected. The QUBO formulation is expressive enough to encode a wide variety of combinatorial optimization tasks, such as portfolio optimization [15], logistics, and scheduling [3]. Moreover, QUBO provides a unified mathematical framework that can be efficiently solved using classical heuristics or specialized hardware, including quantum annealers and Ising-based solvers.

4 QUBO-Based Informative Subset Selection (QUBISS)

We formulate the data subset selection task for efficient fine-tuning of Vision–Language Models (VLMs) as a Quadratic Unconstrained Binary Optimization (QUBO) problem. The overall workflow, illustrated in Fig. 1 and summarized in Algorithm 1, comprises three main stages: (1) extracting task vectors that capture reasoning-relevant semantics for each image–text pair (Sect. 4.1); (2) clustering the representations to reduce problem dimensionality (Sect. 4.2); and (3) solving a QUBO problem within each cluster to select an informative and diverse subset that balances utility and redundancy (Sect. 4.3).

4.1 Feature Extraction

We first represent each image–text pair as a dense feature vector. To obtain interleaved representations that jointly encode visual and textual information, we employ a feature extractor capable of integrating both modalities, rather than treating them independently. We then describe two approaches for this integration: a naive approach and a task-vector-based approach.

Naive Approach. In the naive approach, we directly obtain a single feature vector from each image–text pair using a feature extractor. The model jointly embeds the image and text into a shared latent space, producing a unified representation that captures the overall semantic meaning of the pair.

Task-Vector-Based Approach. To better capture task-specific and reasoning-oriented information, we introduce the task vector representation. As illustrated in Fig. 2, a task vector is computed as the difference between two related embeddings produced by the feature extractor:

1. **Target vector**: obtained from the original image–text pair, with the text including a summarization instruction such as "Summarize the image and text in one word."
2. **Reference vector**: obtained from the same image paired with a generic caption, where all specific question–answer content is replaced by a neutral phrase such as "Look at this image." The summarization instruction is also concatenated.

Algorithm 1: QUBO-based Informative Subset Selection (QUBISS)

Input: Dataset $\mathcal{D} = \{(z_i, c_i)\}_{i=1}^N$, where z_i and c_i denote the image and its text (conversation);

Feature extractor f returning a d-dimensional vector;

Vague instruction c^{vague};

Summarization instruction c^*;

Weight parameters $w_1, w_2 \geq 0$;

Number of clusters M;

Clustering function

$g : (\mathbb{R}^d)^N \times \mathbb{N} \to \{(\mathcal{C}_1, \ldots, \mathcal{C}_M) \mid \mathcal{C}_m \subseteq \{1, \ldots, N\}, \bigsqcup_{m=1}^M \mathcal{C}_m = \{1, \ldots, N\}\}$

Output: Selected informative subset $\mathcal{D}^*$

```
// Step 1: Compute task vectors
```

foreach *instance* $(z_i, c_i) \in \mathcal{D}$ **do**

$\quad e_i^{\mathrm{orig}} \leftarrow f(z_i, c_i \| c^*)$;   `// || denotes string concatenation`

$\quad e_i^{\mathrm{vague}} \leftarrow f(z_i, c^{\mathrm{vague}} \| c^*)$;

$\quad v_i \leftarrow e_i^{\mathrm{orig}} - e_i^{\mathrm{vague}}$; `// Task vector capturing fine-grained semantics`

```
// Step 2: Cluster task vectors to reduce QUBO size
```

$\{\mathcal{C}_1, \mathcal{C}_2, \ldots, \mathcal{C}_M\} \leftarrow g(\{v_i\}_{i=1}^N, M)$;

```
// Step 3: Solve QUBO within each cluster
```

$\mathcal{D}^* \leftarrow \emptyset$;

foreach *cluster* $\mathcal{C}_m$ *in* $\{\mathcal{C}_1, \ldots, \mathcal{C}_M\}$ **do**

$\quad N_m \leftarrow |\mathcal{C}_m|$;

$\quad$ Define a bijection $\iota_m : \mathcal{C}_m \to \{1, \ldots, N_m\}$; `// Relabel global indices in` $\mathcal{C}_m$ `to local indices`

$\quad$ Let $\iota_m^{-1} : \{1, \ldots, N_m\} \to \mathcal{C}_m$ be its inverse ;   `// Exists since` ι_m `is a bijection`

$\quad$ Initialize $Q^{(m)} \in \mathbb{R}^{N_m \times N_m}$ with zeros;

$\quad$ **foreach** *instance* $i \in \mathcal{C}_m$ **do**

$\quad\quad k \leftarrow \iota_m(i)$;

$\quad\quad Q_{k,k}^{(m)} \leftarrow w_1 \|v_i\|_2$;   `// Utility term: informative samples`

$\quad$ **foreach** *pair* (i, j) *in* $\mathcal{C}_m$, $i < j$ **do**

$\quad\quad k \leftarrow \iota_m(i)$;

$\quad\quad l \leftarrow \iota_m(j)$;

$\quad\quad Q_{k,l}^{(m)} \leftarrow -w_2 \cdot \dfrac{v_i \cdot v_j}{\|v_i\|_2 \|v_j\|_2}$;   `// Redundancy term: pairwise similarity penalty`

$\quad\quad Q_{l,k}^{(m)} \leftarrow Q_{k,l}^{(m)}$;

```
// Solve the local QUBO and map selected local indices back to
   global samples
```

$\quad x^{(m)*} \leftarrow \arg\max_{x \in \{0,1\}^{N_m}} x^\top Q^{(m)} x$;

$\quad \mathcal{D}^* \leftarrow \mathcal{D}^* \cup \{(z_{\iota_m^{-1}(k)}, c_{\iota_m^{-1}(k)}) \mid x_k^{(m)*} = 1,\ k = 1, \ldots, N_m\}$;

---

return $\mathcal{D}^*$

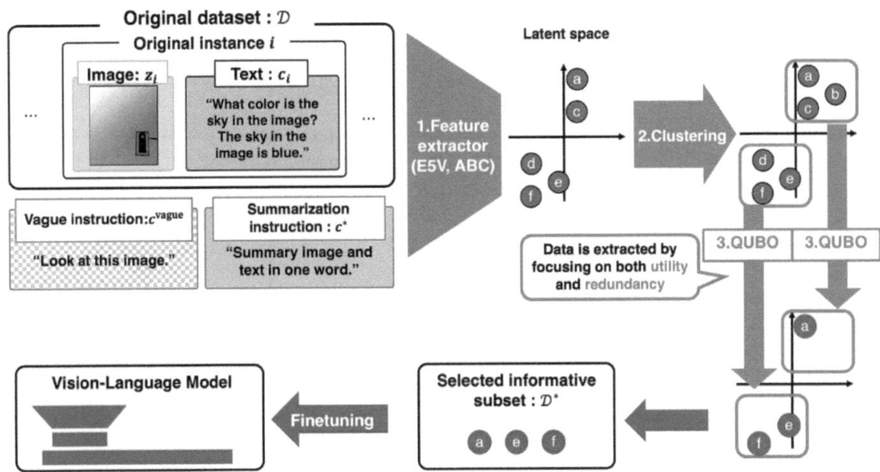

Fig. 1. Overview of the proposed QUBO-based Informative Subset Selection (QUBISS). The method computes task vectors from paired embeddings, clusters them to reduce the QUBO problem size, and solves cluster-wise QUBO problems to select an informative and diverse subset.

The difference between these two vectors effectively isolates the fine-grained semantic information that is lost in the vague version. Thus, the task vector emphasizes the unique reasoning-relevant contribution of each instance, providing a more discriminative feature representation for subsequent selection.

For this purpose, we explore two approaches, both leveraging powerful vision–language encoders: E5-V [9] and ABC [18]. E5-V adapts multimodal large language models to produce universal multimodal embeddings through a prompt-based feature extraction strategy. By unifying text and image representations into a shared embedding space with simple guiding prompts (e.g., "summarize in one word"), E5-V enables the model to represent multimodal inputs consistently without requiring multimodal fine-tuning. Trained only on text pairs, it achieves strong performance on retrieval and composition tasks by transferring single-modality language understanding to multimodal representation learning.

An alternative approach utilizes ABC [18]. ABC is a fine-tuned multimodal embedding model that extends a VLM to control visual embeddings through natural language instructions. By conditioning image representations on text prompts, it allows users to focus on specific regions or aspects of an image, enabling fine-grained and interpretable control over visual features. This approach achieves strong performance across retrieval, classification, and visual question answering tasks by deeply integrating language guidance into visual representation learning.

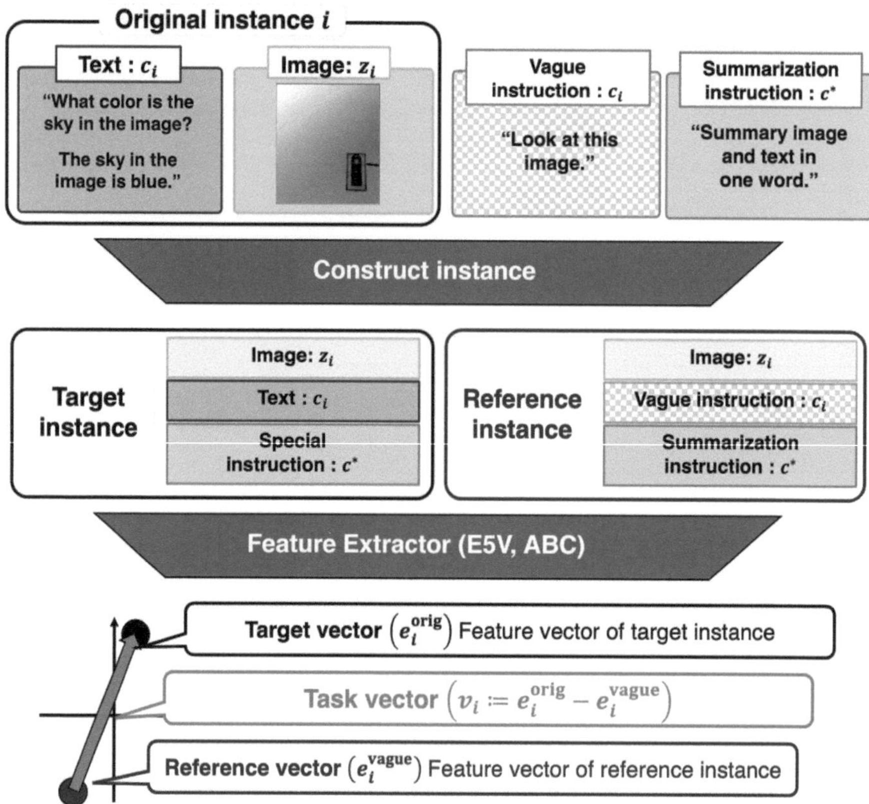

Fig. 2. Illustration of the task vector calculation. It is defined as the difference between the embedding of an original, descriptive instance and that of an instance in which the text has been replaced with vague information, referred to as the reference instance.

4.2 Clustering

The original dataset typically contains a large number of instances, making the direct application of combinatorial optimization computationally intractable. To mitigate this, we employ the k-means algorithm to partition the dataset into a manageable number of clusters. By grouping the extracted feature or task vectors into M clusters (e.g., $M = 100$), the subsequent optimization can be performed independently within each cluster. This strategy substantially reduces the search space while maintaining the representativeness of the overall dataset, thereby ensuring computational tractability.

4.3 Optimization

The core of our approach is to formulate subset selection within each cluster as a Quadratic Unconstrained Binary Optimization (QUBO) problem that explicitly balances utility and redundancy. The goal is to find a binary selection vector $\boldsymbol{x}$ that maximizes the following quadratic objective:

$$\max_{\boldsymbol{x} \in \{0,1\}^{N_m}} \boldsymbol{x}^\top Q^{(m)} \boldsymbol{x}, \tag{3}$$

where N_m denotes the size of the m-th cluster, and each element x_i is defined as

$$x_i = \begin{cases} 1, & \text{if instance } i \text{ is selected for fine-tuning,} \\ 0, & \text{otherwise.} \end{cases}$$

The QUBO matrix $Q^{(m)}$ corresponding to cluster m encodes both instance-level utility and pairwise redundancy as follows:

$$Q_{i,j}^{(m)} = \begin{cases} w_1 \left\| \boldsymbol{v}_i \right\|_2, & (i = j), \\ -w_2 \dfrac{\langle \boldsymbol{v}_i, \boldsymbol{v}_j \rangle}{\left\| \boldsymbol{v}_i \right\|_2 \left\| \boldsymbol{v}_j \right\|_2}, & (i \neq j), \end{cases}$$

where $w_1, w_2 > 0$ are balancing coefficients, and $\left\| \boldsymbol{v}_i \right\|_2$ denotes the ℓ_2 norm of the feature (or task) vector $\boldsymbol{v}_i$.

- **Utility (Diagonal terms):** The diagonal elements $Q_{i,i}$ represent the *utility* of selecting instance i. This term is defined by the norm of its feature vector $\left\| \boldsymbol{v}_i \right\|_2$, which prioritizes instances with larger magnitudes—presumed to encode more fine-grained and informative content. This formulation is motivated by findings that embedding norms correlate with information richness [16].
- **Redundancy (Off-diagonal terms):** The off-diagonal elements $Q_{i,j}$ serve as a redundancy penalty, defined as the negative cosine similarity between $\boldsymbol{v}_i$ and $\boldsymbol{v}_j$. If two instances are highly similar, selecting both incurs a large penalty, thereby discouraging redundant information in the final subset.

Maximizing this objective yields a subset that jointly maximizes informativeness and diversity. The hyperparameters w_1 and w_2 control the relative trade-off between these two competing objectives.

5   Numerical Experiments

This section presents the experimental setup in Sect. 5.1 and reports the results in Sect. 5.2. The ablation study is presented in Sect. 5.3. Our experiments are designed to investigate whether the dataset selected by QUBISS is effective compared with existing baselines.

5.1   Experimental Settings

To evaluate the effectiveness of our QUBO-based subset selection method, we conduct experiments on a multimodal evaluation (MME) task. Note that all text-only samples are included during fine-tuning to prevent performance degradation. Therefore, the data selection algorithm is applied only to instances that contain both image and text modalities.

- **Dataset:** We begin with the large-scale LLaVA-665K [13] instruction dataset, which contains 665,298 instances.
- **Base Model:** We adopt a LLaVA-like architecture as the base Vision–Language Model, combining a pretrained ViT-L/14 as the visual encoder [17] with Vicuna-7B as the pretrained language model.
- **Feature Extraction and Clustering:** Feature vectors for each instance are extracted using E5-V [9] or ABC [18], as described in Sect. 4.1. The number of clusters for k-means is set to $M = 100$, following the default configuration.
- **Baselines for Comparison:** We compare our approach with four baselines:
  1. **Random subset selection:** A naive baseline that randomly samples a subset of the same size as that selected by QUBISS.
  2. **CLIP** [17]: CLIP is utilized as the feature extractor. Text and image features are obtained independently and then concatenated. When the number of tokens produced by the CLIP tokenizer exceeds the model's maximum token limit, we divide the text into smaller chunks, extract embeddings for each chunk using the CLIP text encoder, and then average these embeddings to obtain the final text representation.
  3. **BLIP2** [12]: BLIP2 is also utilized as the feature extractor. Similar to CLIP, text and image features are extracted independently and concatenated. When the number of tokens produced by the tokenizer exceeds the model's maximum token limit, the text is divided into smaller chunks, and the embeddings obtained from each chunk are averaged to form the final text representation.
  4. **COINCIDE** [11]: A state-of-the-art VLM data selection method that minimizes cluster-level distribution discrepancy between subsets and the full dataset. The subset size is matched to that of QUBISS.
- **Implementation Details:** Fine-tuning is performed for a fixed number of epochs with a constant learning rate. The QUBO weights are set to $w_1 = 0.6$ and $w_2 = 0.1$ when using E5-V to manually restrict the number of extracted data samples to an appropriate level.
- **Evaluation Metric:** Model performance is evaluated using the Multimodal Evaluation (MME) benchmark [6]. It consists of perception tests (MME-P) and cognition tests (MME-C). MME-P comprises eight perception-oriented categories, whereas MME-C includes four cognition-oriented ones. Each category contains multiple yes/no question–answer pairs.
- **Computational Environment:** All experiments are conducted on a server equipped with four NVIDIA A100 GPUs (80 GB each).

– **Solver:** The Gurobi Optimizer (v12.0.2) is used to solve the QUBO problem. The time limit is set to 300 s with 10 threads. As future work, we plan to explore quantum computing-based solvers.

5.2   Results and Discussion

The results of our experiments, summarized in Table 1, demonstrate the effectiveness of the proposed QUBO-based subset selection method. Our approach not only achieves performance competitive with fine-tuning on the full dataset but also significantly outperforms standard baseline selection methods. For the QUBO problems, we obtained optimal solutions in 90 out of 100 instances when using E5-V as the feature extractor.

Table 1. Comparison of MME-P and MME-C scores across different dataset selection methods. Under the QUBISS w/o task vector setting, we employ the naive approach without acquiring the reference vector. The best results are highlighted in bold.

Methods	Feature extractor	MME-P ($\uparrow$)	MME-C ($\uparrow$)
Random	-	1,385	315
CLIP [17]	CLIP	1,284	248
BLIP2 [12]	BLIP2	1,311	277
COINCIDE [11]	LLaVA v1.5	**1,504**	286
QUBISS	E5-V	1,336	**349**
QUBISS w/o task vector	E5-V	1,435	301
QUBISS	ABC	1,364	290
QUBISS w/o task vector	ABC	1,356	289

Quantitative Evaluation. We conducted a quantitative evaluation to compare the performance of our proposed method against the COINCIDE baseline, focusing on both perceptual and cognitive capabilities. Our proposed framework, QUBISS, inherently incorporates a *task vector* that guides the optimization toward cognitively meaningful representations. To assess its contribution, we additionally conduct an ablation study by removing this component, denoted as QUBISS w/o task vector. As shown in Table 1, the QUBISS model achieves a higher MME-C score of 349 compared to 301 without the task vector, indicating a clear improvement in reasoning-oriented performance. This enhancement comes with a moderate decrease in perception-oriented performance (MME-P: 1,336 vs. 1,435), reflecting a controlled shift of representational focus from perceptual fidelity toward cognitive abstraction. In comparison, while COINCIDE [11] achieves the best MME-P score of 1,504, QUBISS exhibits stronger reasoning capability, surpassing COINCIDE on the MME-C benchmark (349 vs. 286).

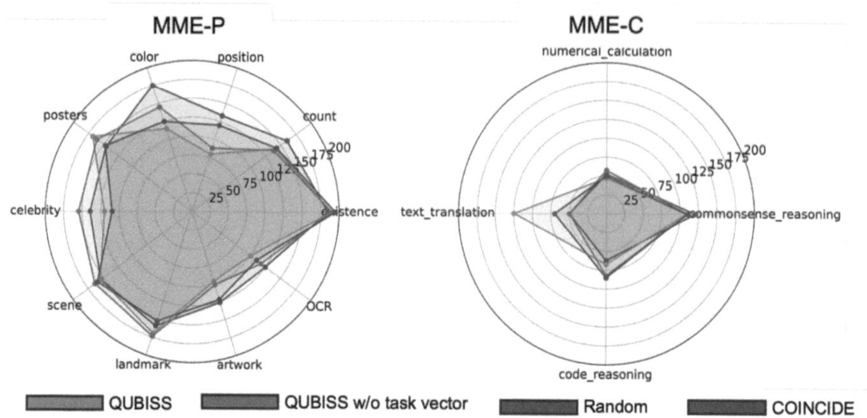

Fig. 3. Radar chart illustrating the detailed performance reported in Table 1. MME-P and MME-C are designed to evaluate perception and cognition performance, respectively.

As shown in Fig. 3, QUBISS consistently outperforms the baselines across both perception-type (MME-P) and cognition-type (MME-C) benchmarks. In MME-P, the improvement is particularly notable for the landmark and poster categories, demonstrating that QUBISS effectively enhances discriminative visual representations through informative subset selection. The method also maintains stable performance in the scene and landmark categories, indicating that the selected samples preserve contextual diversity. In contrast, the gains are smaller for color and position, suggesting that tasks involving textual or abstract understanding benefit less from purely visual data selection. QUBISS likely suffered a performance drop in areas involving proper nouns—such as celebrity names—because its data selection process prioritized the capabilities required to answer each instance, resulting in insufficient coverage of the content handled across instances.

For MME-C, the overall scores are lower across all methods, reflecting the inherent difficulty of cognition-oriented reasoning tasks. QUBISS shows slight advantages in commonsense reasoning and text translation, implying that its selection process retains semantically diverse content. However, in code reasoning and numerical calculation, the gap between QUBISS and Random is marginal, revealing that task-vector-based selection alone cannot capture structured or symbolic reasoning patterns. The ablation study (QUBISS w/o task vector) further supports this observation: ignoring the task vector leads to performance degradation, especially in color and position. This indicates that task vectors play a crucial role in separating task-specific subspaces and emphasizing locally informative features.

Overall, QUBISS provides clear benefits for cognition-focused tasks by improving the diversity and informativeness of selected samples. Nevertheless, its limited gains in high-level reasoning tasks suggest that incorporating structured task representations or hierarchical reasoning cues will be an important direction for future work.

Fig. 4. Sample image extracted from the Japanese-Heron-Bench. The input text prompt is: "What should the driver do next?"

Qualitative Evaluation. Beyond quantitative metrics, we observed qualitative improvements in the model's reasoning capabilities. A sample image is shown in Fig. 4, which is included in the Japanese-Heron-Bench [8]. Responses generated by the trained model are presented in Table 2.

The COINCIDE baseline tends to produce generic descriptions that primarily rely on obvious visual cues (e.g., traffic lights or signs) without considering contextual dependencies, such as the presence of a construction worker actively controlling traffic. The Random baseline identifies both key elements—the signal and the worker—but does not clearly prioritize the worker's guidance over the traffic light. In contrast, QUBISS accurately captures the critical contextual element—the man with the red flag—and correctly infers his role as a traffic controller. This indicates that QUBISS effectively leverages informative features to associate local object relationships (e.g., human posture, safety gear, and cones) with the underlying task semantics, leading to more situation-aware reasoning.

Meanwhile, QUBISS w/o task vector produces a partially correct yet incomplete interpretation by focusing solely on the red signal while overlooking the dynamic instruction implied by the human operator. This demonstrates that the task vector plays an essential role in guiding the model toward task-relevant contextual reasoning rather than static object perception. Overall, these results support our claim that QUBISS enhances interpretability and contextual alignment by integrating task-aware feature selection into the reasoning process.

Table 2. Qualitative evaluation using the sample instance shown in Fig. 4. Under the QUBISS w/o task vector setting, we employ the naive approach without acquiring the reference vector.

Methods	Output
Random	The driver should proceed with caution and be prepared to stop at the intersection. There are several traffic lights present, indicating that the intersection is controlled by traffic signals. The man in the yellow vest is standing near the road, possibly directing traffic or ensuring safety. **The driver should pay attention to the traffic lights and follow the instructions given by the man in the yellow vest to ensure a smooth and safe passage through the intersection.**
COINCIDE	The driver should follow the traffic signs and signals, which include the red stop sign and the yellow arrow pointing to the right. The stop sign indicates that the driver should come to a complete stop before proceeding. The yellow arrow suggests that the driver should turn right at the intersection. By following these signs and signals, the driver can ensure their safety and the safety of others on the road.
QUBISS (E5-V)	In the image, a man is standing on the side of the road, holding a red flag, and there are several traffic cones and signs nearby. The driver should approach the man with the red flag and follow his instructions. The man might be directing traffic or signaling the driver to stop or proceed in a specific direction. **The driver should pay attention to the man's actions and follow his guidance to ensure the safety of all road users and maintain smooth traffic flow.**
QUBISS w/o task vector (E5-V)	The driver should stop at the red traffic light, as it is currently showing a red signal. The worker in the safety vest is standing near the traffic light, indicating that it is a construction zone. **The driver should wait for the traffic light to turn green before proceeding, ensuring their safety and the safety of the construction workers.**

5.3   Ablation Study

To further examine the effect of the feature extractor used to compute the diagonal elements of our metric, we conducted an ablation study in which we replaced only this extractor while keeping the off-diagonal extractor fixed. Table 3 summarizes the results. Using BLIP-2 to compute the diagonal features yielded the

Table 3. Ablation study evaluating the effect of changing the feature extractor for the diagonal elements. The best results are highlighted in bold.

Feature extractor (for off-diagonal elements)	Feature extractor (for diagonal elements)	MME-P ($\uparrow$)	MME-C ($\uparrow$)
E5-V w/o task vector	E5-V w/o task vector	1,435	301
E5-V w/o task vector	E5-V	1,347	311
E5-V w/o task vector	ABC w/o task vector	1,392	301
E5-V w/o task vector	ABC	1,358	250
E5-V w/o task vector	BLIP2	**1,450**	**325**

best performance, improving MME-P from 1,435 to 1,450 and MME-C from 301 to 325. This suggests that BLIP-2's strong vision–language alignment produces more discriminative self-representations and stabilizes the diagonal terms of the metric. In contrast, substituting the feature extractor for the diagonal elements with models lacking such alignment (e.g., E5-V w/o task vector) resulted in lower consistency scores, indicating that the choice of feature extractor substantially influences the reliability of the metric.

6   Conclusion

In this work, we presented QUBO-based Informative Subset Selection (QUBISS), a novel framework for efficient fine-tuning of Vision–Language Models (VLMs) through task-aware data subset selection. QUBISS formulates the subset selection process as a Quadratic Unconstrained Binary Optimization (QUBO) problem that jointly optimizes data utility and redundancy, thereby constructing a compact yet highly informative training subset. A key component of QUBISS is the introduction of the task vector, an advanced feature representation that captures reasoning-relevant semantics by contrasting an image–text pair with its de-specified counterpart. This task-sensitive formulation embeds fine-grained cognitive information directly into the QUBO utility term, allowing the framework to prioritize data instances that contribute most to reasoning performance. Our numerical experiments validate the effectiveness of QUBISS: fine-tuning on subsets selected by the proposed method achieves performance comparable to full-dataset training while using only a fraction of the data, and surpasses standard baselines such as random selection and COINCIDE.

For future work, several directions remain open. First, developing adaptive parameter search strategies for the QUBO formulation could further improve selection efficiency. Second, we plan to evaluate QUBISS across broader datasets and architectures to assess its generality. Finally, leveraging quantum solvers for large-scale QUBO optimization may enable substantial acceleration. Large-scale solvers could further improve the quality of the selected dataset by enabling QUBISS to formulate dataset selection as a single QUBO, thereby eliminating the reliance on k-means clustering and mitigating the risk of suboptimal solutions arising from problem decomposition.

Acknowledgments. This research project was supported by the Japan Science and Technology Agency (JST), the Core Research of Evolutionary Science and Technology (CREST), and JSPS KAKENHI Grant Number JP21H04599, Japan.

References

1. Chen, R., et al.: Your vision-language model itself is a strong filter: towards high-quality instruction tuning with data selection. In: Findings of the Association for Computational Linguistics: ACL 2024 (2024)
2. Chiang, W.L., et al.: Vicuna: an open-source chatbot impressing gpt-4 with 90%* chatgpt quality (2023). https://lmsys.org/blog/2023-03-30-vicuna/
3. Debevere, P., Sugimura, M., Parizy, M.: Quadratic unconstrained binary optimization for the automotive paint shop problem. IEEE Access **11**, 97769–97777 (2023)
4. Feng, L., Nie, F., Liu, Y., Alahi, A.: TAROT: targeted data selection via optimal transport. In: Proceedings of the 42nd International Conference on Machine Learning, pp. 16837–16852 (2025)
5. Feuer, B., Xu, J., Cohen, N., Yubeaton, P., Mittal, G., Hegde, C.: Select: a large-scale benchmark of data curation strategies for image classification. Adv. Neural. Inf. Process. Syst. **37**, 136620–136645 (2024)
6. Fu, C., et al.: MME: a comprehensive evaluation benchmark for multimodal large language models (2024). https://arxiv.org/abs/2306.13394
7. Gadre, S.Y., et al.: Datacomp: in search of the next generation of multimodal datasets. Adv. Neural. Inf. Process. Syst. **36**, 27092–27112 (2023)
8. Inoue, Y., Sasaki, K., Ochi, Y., Fujii, K., Tanahashi, K., Yamaguchi, Y.: Heron-bench: a benchmark for evaluating vision language models in Japanese. arXiv preprint arXiv:2404.07824 (2024)
9. Jiang, T., et al.: E5-v: universal embeddings with multimodal large language models. arXiv preprint arXiv:2407.12580 (2024)
10. Lee, H., Kim, S., Lee, J., Yoo, J., Kwak, N.: Coreset selection for object detection. In: Proceedings of the IEEE/CVF Conference on Computer Vision and Pattern Recognition, pp. 7682–7691 (2024)
11. Lee, J., Li, B., Hwang, S.J.: Concept-skill transferability-based data selection for large vision-language models. In: Proceedings of the 2024 Conference on Empirical Methods in Natural Language Processing, pp. 5060–5080 (2024)
12. Li, J., Li, D., Savarese, S., Hoi, S.: Blip-2: bootstrapping language-image pre-training with frozen image encoders and large language models. In: International Conference on Machine Learning, pp. 19730–19742. PMLR (2023)
13. Liu, H., Li, C., Li, Y., Lee, Y.J.: Improved baselines with visual instruction tuning. In: Proceedings of the IEEE/CVF Conference on Computer Vision and Pattern Recognition, pp. 26296–26306 (2024)
14. Liu, H., Li, C., Wu, Q., Lee, Y.J.: Visual instruction tuning. Adv. Neural. Inf. Process. Syst. **36**, 34892–34916 (2023)
15. Lu, Y.C., Fu, C.M., Yu, L.P., Chang, Y.J., Chang, C.R.: Quantum-inspired portfolio optimization in the qubo framework. arXiv preprint arXiv:2410.05932 (2024)

16. Oyama, M., Yokoi, S., Shimodaira, H.: Norm of word embedding encodes information gain. In: Proceedings of the 2023 Conference on Empirical Methods in Natural Language Processing (2023)
17. Radford, A., et al.: Learning transferable visual models from natural language supervision. In: International Conference on Machine Learning, pp. 8748–8763. PmLR (2021)
18. Schneider, B., Kerschbaum, F., Chen, W.: ABC: achieving better control of visual embeddings using vllms. Trans. Mach. Learn. Res. (2025)
19. Shen, Y., et al.: ProcTag: process tagging for assessing the efficacy of document instruction data. In: Proceedings of the AAAI Conference on Artificial Intelligence, vol. 39, pp. 6851–6859 (2025)
20. Sorscher, B., Geirhos, R., Shekhar, S., Ganguli, S., Morcos, A.: Beyond neural scaling laws: beating power law scaling via data pruning. Adv. Neural. Inf. Process. Syst. **35**, 19523–19536 (2022)
21. Spravil, J., Houben, S., Behnke, S.: Florenz: scaling laws for systematic generalization in vision-language models. arXiv preprint arXiv:2503.09443 (2025)
22. Tirumala, K., Simig, D., Aghajanyan, A., Morcos, A.: D4: Improving LLM pre-training via document de-duplication and diversification. Adv. Neural. Inf. Process. Syst. **36**, 53983–53995 (2023)
23. Touvron, H., et al.: Llama 2: open foundation and fine-tuned chat models (2023)
24. Wu, X., Xia, M., Shao, R., Deng, Z., Koh, P.W., Russakovsky, O.: Icons: influence consensus for vision-language data selection. arXiv preprint arXiv:2501.00654 (2024)
25. Zhang, J., Qin, Y., Pi, R., Zhang, W., Pan, R., Zhang, T.: TAGCOS: task-agnostic gradient clustered coreset selection for instruction tuning data. In: Findings of the Association for Computational Linguistics: NAACL 2025, pp. 4671–4686 (2025)
26. Zhao, H., Du, L., Ju, Y., Wu, C., Pan, T.: Beyond IID: optimizing instruction fine-tuning from the perspective of instruction interaction and dependency. In: Proceedings of the AAAI Conference on Artificial Intelligence, vol. 39, no. 24, pp. 26031–26038 (2025)
27. Zhou, C., et al.: Lima: less is more for alignment. Adv. Neural. Inf. Process. Syst. **36**, 55006–55021 (2023)

Hybrid Learning and Optimization Methods for Solving Capacitated Vehicle Routing Problem

Monit Sharma and Hoong Chuin Lau

School of Computing and Information Systems, Singapore Management University,
Singapore, Singapore
{monitsharma,hclau}@smu.edu.sg

Abstract. We propose a hybrid quantum–classical framework for the Capacitated Vehicle Routing Problem (CVRP) that integrates the Augmented Lagrangian Method (ALM) with deep reinforcement learning (RL). Directly solving CVRP via Variational Quantum Eigensolver (VQE) requires a slack-based QUBO formulation, where converting inequalities to equalities greatly increases the qubit count. To circumvent this, we employ an ALM-based reformulation that enforces constraints through Lagrange terms instead of slack variables, drastically reducing quantum resource demands. An RL agent, trained with Soft Actor–Critic, adaptively tunes the Lagrange penalties to improve convergence and feasibility. Experiments show that RL-Q-ALM outperforms static-penalty and plain VQE baselines in both solution quality and convergence stability, demonstrating RL's potential for scalable, adaptive quantum optimization (Code available at: https://github.com/SMU-Quantum/adaptive_quantum_cvrp).

Keywords: Capacitated Vehicle Routing Problem · Augmented Lagrangian Method · Reinforcement Learning · Soft Actor-Critic · Quantum Optimization · Variational Quantum Eigensolver · QUBO · Hybrid Quantum-Classical Computing

1 Introduction

The Capacitated Vehicle Routing Problem (CVRP) is a longstanding benchmark in combinatorial optimization, central to logistics and transportation planning [1,2,11]. Despite decades of progress, exact and heuristic algorithms continue to face scalability challenges due to the problem's NP-hard nature [17,18]. Classical approaches, while effective on moderate instances, often rely on manual parameter tuning and domain heuristics [19,20], limiting their adaptability across problem scales and structures.

In parallel, two emerging paradigms, reinforcement learning (RL) and quantum optimization, offer complementary strengths. RL enables adaptive, instance-aware decision-making by learning from experience [21], while quantum algorithms such as the Variational Quantum Eigensolver (VQE) [12] promise new

© The Author(s), under exclusive license to Springer Nature Switzerland AG 2026
S. Ali et al. (Eds.): QC+AI 2026, CCIS 2872, pp. 18–33, 2026.
https://doi.org/10.1007/978-3-032-17625-7_2

ways to explore combinatorial landscapes [22,24,25]. Yet, each faces limitations: RL policies can struggle with constraint satisfaction, and near-term quantum devices remain restricted by noise and circuit depth.

This work proposes a unifying direction: embedding RL within a classical–quantum optimization framework to create *learning-augmented quantum solvers*. Building on the Augmented Lagrangian Method (ALM) [4,5], we develop a hybrid architecture where RL adaptively tunes the penalty parameters that guides the quantum subproblem solvers. For the purpose of comparison, we will study the following approaches:

- **C-ALM** (baseline 1) this is a purely classical approach using Lagrange multipliers and penalties;
- **VQE** (baseline 2) this is a purely quantum approach using Variational Quantum Eigensolver on a standard Quadratic Unconstrained Binary Optimization (QUBO) formulation;
- **Q-ALM** solves a QUBO augmented Langragian formulation and using VQE; and
- **RL-Q-ALM** combines RL with Q-ALM in a single feedback loop.

By hybridizing AI with quantum optimization, this study moves beyond algorithmic comparison toward a cohesive paradigm for adaptive, scalable, and intelligent hybrid solvers. Benchmark results on synthetic and standard CVRPLIB datasets [23] demonstrate how learning-driven parameter control can enhance convergence and solution quality across both classical and quantum domains.

1.1   The Capacitated Vehicle Routing Problem

Let $V = \{0, 1, \ldots, n\}$ denote the nodes, with 0 as the depot and $\{1, \ldots, n\}$ as customers. Each customer i has demand $d_i \geq 0$, and each vehicle $k \in K$ has capacity Q. The travel cost between nodes i and j is c_{ij}. A feasible solution consists of vehicle routes such that: (i) each customer is visited once, (ii) every route starts and ends at the depot, and (iii) the total demand per route does not exceed Q. The goal is to minimize the total travel cost.

We employ the three-index vehicle-flow ILP with Miller–Tucker–Zemlin (MTZ) subtour elimination constraints [11].

Decision variables.

$$x_{ijk} = \begin{cases} 1 & \text{if vehicle } k \text{ travels from } i \text{ to } j, \\ 0 & \text{otherwise} \end{cases} \qquad \forall i, j \in V,\, i \neq j,\, k \in K$$

$$u_{ik} = \text{load on vehicle } k \text{ after visiting } i, \quad i \in \{1, \ldots, n\},\, k \in K$$

Objective.

$$\min \sum_{k \in K} \sum_{i \in V} \sum_{\substack{j \in V \\ j \neq i}} c_{ij} x_{ijk}$$

Constraints.

$$\sum_{k \in K} \sum_{\substack{i \in V \\ i \neq j}} x_{ijk} = 1 \qquad \forall j \in \{1, \ldots, n\} \qquad \text{(Customer visit)}$$

$$\sum_{j=1}^{n} x_{0jk} = 1, \quad \sum_{i=1}^{n} x_{i0k} = 1 \qquad \forall k \in K \qquad \text{(Depot depart/return)}$$

$$\sum_{\substack{i \in V \\ i \neq j}} x_{ijk} = \sum_{\substack{l \in V \\ l \neq j}} x_{jlk} \qquad \forall j, k \qquad \text{(Flow conservation)}$$

$$\sum_{i=1}^{n} d_i \sum_{\substack{j \in V \\ j \neq i}} x_{ijk} \leq Q \qquad \forall k \in K \qquad \text{(Capacity)}$$

$$u_{ik} + d_j \leq u_{jk} + Q(1 - x_{ijk}), \quad d_i \leq u_{ik} \leq Q, \quad u_{ik} \geq d_i \sum_{j=0}^{n} x_{jik} \quad \text{(MTZ)}$$

Constraint (MTZ) enforces load consistency and prevents subtours, while bounding and activating u_{ik} appropriately. Constraint (Capacity) is theoretically redundant but strengthens the LP relaxation.

Domain.

$$x_{ijk} \in \{0, 1\}, \quad u_{ik} \in \mathbb{R}_+, \quad \forall i, j, k$$

Complexity. The CVRP is strongly NP-hard [17], with search space growing factorially in n and combinatorially in $|K|$. Hence, exact algorithms become infeasible beyond moderate sizes ($n \gtrsim 50$), motivating approximation, learning-based, and hybrid methods.

1.2   Key Contributions

This work bridges operations research, quantum computing, and reinforcement learning to answer a central question: how can quantum and learning-based techniques be meaningfully embedded within classical frameworks to solve structured NP-hard problems like CVRP? Unlike prior quantum studies on synthetic QUBOs, we anchor quantum solvers in a real-world logistics setting, integrating them with ALM and RL to ensure adaptability, and constraint feasibility on NISQ devices.

Our main contributions are:

- **Methodological Innovation:** We propose three integrated solvers: (i) **C-ALM**, a structure-aware Augmented Lagrangian formulation for CVRP; (ii) **Q-ALM**, which embeds quantum variational solvers (VQE/QAOA) into the ALM pipeline through QUBO reformulation; and (iii) **RL-Q-ALM**, combining reinforcement learning–based penalty adaptation with quantum subproblem solving for scalable constraint satisfaction.

- **Empirical Evaluation:** Extensive benchmarks across standard CVRP instances compare all four methods on solution quality, feasibility, circuit depth, robustness to shot noise, and scalability across problem sizes.
- **Cross-Domain Generality:** The RL-Quantum framework extends beyond CVRP to other constrained combinatorial tasks (e.g., scheduling, portfolio optimization), offering a transferable blueprint for RL-tuned QUBO solvers in real-world applications.

2   Literature Review

2.1   Augmented Lagrangian Methods for CVRP

Augmented Lagrangian Methods (ALM) integrate Lagrange multipliers with quadratic penalties to handle constraints effectively [3–7]. By alternating between minimizing an augmented objective and updating multipliers, ALM balances feasibility and numerical stability better than pure penalty methods. For convex problems, convergence is well understood; in discrete settings, ALM's success relies on decomposition and heuristic updates [13].

In routing problems, ALM can relax global constraints, such as assignment, capacity, and routing feasibility, enabling decomposition into tractable subproblems, closely related to Lagrangian relaxation and column-generation frameworks [14,15]. Dualizing customer or capacity constraints turns each vehicle subproblem into an Elementary Shortest Path Problem with Resource Constraints (ESP-PRC), solvable via dynamic programming or labeling for moderate sizes [27–29]. ADMM-style decompositions have further extended ALM to distributed VRP formulations [16].

For CVRP, performance depends on three design elements: decomposition, penalty scheduling, and multiplier updates. We adopt standard update rules [4,5,30], where multipliers are adjusted proportionally to constraint violations. Managing the penalty parameter ρ_k is critical, low values slow convergence, while high values cause instability. Adaptive updates increase ρ_k when violation stagnates and decrease it when subproblems diverge [3,26,30]. Later, we extend this idea with reinforcement learning to learn penalty schedules directly from instance features [31].

Although convergence guarantees are limited in discrete domains, ALM remains valuable as a hybrid coordination layer. Intermediate iterates often yield high-quality, near-feasible routes that seed heuristics or exact methods [32–34]. In our framework, these iterates and multipliers provide informative signals, penalties, duals, and residuals, that guide reinforcement learning and quantum solvers, establishing ALM as a unifying foundation for adaptive and quantum-assisted CVRP optimization.

2.2   Reinforcement Learning for Adaptive Parameter Tuning in Optimization

The performance of Augmented Lagrangian Methods (ALM) in solving structured problems such as CVRP depends critically on penalty coefficients that balance feasibility and objective quality. Conventional tuning relies on heuristic or fixed schedules [35,37], which are often instance-specific and sensitive to initialization. Reinforcement Learning (RL) offers a data-driven alternative by framing penalty adjustment as a sequential decision process, where an agent interacts with the optimization routine, observes features such as constraint violation or dual gradients, and selects actions corresponding to updated penalty parameters [38–40]. The agent is rewarded according to convergence speed, solution feasibility, and objective improvement, thereby learning an adaptive policy that generalizes across problem instances [41]. Prior work shows that RL can dynamically tune hyperparameters and multipliers in constrained optimization, improving robustness and efficiency [3,26,31,36].

We follow this paradigm by coupling standard ALM updates [4,5,30] with an RL policy that adaptively selects penalty magnitudes during training. The agent refines penalties online based on constraint satisfaction trends rather than fixed heuristics, automating the trade-off between feasibility and cost. Unlike model-predictive or constraint-masking RL schemes [36,40], our framework preserves ALM's theoretical structure while introducing learning-based adaptivity. This integration treats penalty tuning as a learnable control problem, maintaining convergence guarantees of ALM while improving its responsiveness to instance heterogeneity and non-stationary constraint dynamics.

3   The Classical Augmented Lagrangian Method for CVRP (C-ALM)

The Classical Augmented Lagrangian Method (C-ALM) forms the baseline framework of this study. It formulates the Capacitated Vehicle Routing Problem (CVRP) as a constrained optimization problem, handling routing and capacity constraints through Lagrange multipliers and penalty terms. This classical foundation provides the structure upon which reinforcement learning and quantum enhancements are later built.

3.1   Augmented Lagrangian Formulation for CVRP

We employ the Augmented Lagrangian Method (ALM) by relaxing the two principal CVRP constraints, customer visit and vehicle capacity, through linear multipliers and quadratic penalties. Specifically, let $S = \{R_1, \ldots, R_m\}$ represent a candidate set of routes (with $m \leq K_{\max}$) and $C(S)$ denote the total routing cost. Each customer $j \in C$ is associated with a visit constraint $v_j(S) = 1$, and each route R_k with a capacity constraint $L(R_k) \leq Q$. These are relaxed using multipliers λ_j, μ_k and penalties ρ_j, σ_k, producing an augmented objective that balances cost and feasibility.

The overall objective takes the compact form:

$$L_{\mathrm{aug}}(S) = C(S) + \sum_{j \in C}\left[\lambda_j(v_j(S) - 1) + \tfrac{1}{2}\rho_j(v_j(S) - 1)^2\right] + \sum_{k=1}^{m}\left[\mu_k h_k(S) + \tfrac{1}{2}\sigma_k h_k(S)^2\right], \quad (1)$$

where $h_k(S)$ measures the excess load of route R_k beyond vehicle capacity.

This augmented objective $L_{\mathrm{aug}}(S)$ is minimized iteratively: routes are optimized with fixed multipliers and penalties, then λ, μ and ρ, σ are updated based on constraint violations, following standard ALM updates [3–5]. In effect, ALM converts the constrained CVRP into a sequence of unconstrained subproblems whose penalties enforce customer coverage and capacity feasibility while allowing temporary violations that guide search toward high-quality feasible solutions.

3.2 Subproblem Generation: Route Construction via ESP

At each ALM iteration, routes are constructed by solving an Elementary Shortest Path (ESP) problem over the customer set with modified costs derived from the current multipliers. The relaxed customer-visit constraints introduce dual terms λ_j that act as node rewards: customers with higher λ_j (i.e., those insufficiently served) become more attractive to include in a route. Concretely, we assign each customer a reward of $-\lambda_j$ and run a shortest-path heuristic from the depot to itself to generate elementary depot-to-depot tours, balancing travel cost against dual incentives [27, 28].

This procedure yields up to $K_{\max}$ candidate routes per iteration. Customers already visited are excluded from subsequent subproblems to encourage route diversity. Capacity multipliers μ_k and penalties σ_k are evaluated afterward within the global augmented objective and thus do not influence the local ESP construction directly. Subtours are avoided by design, as each ESP solution forms a single elementary depot-anchored path. In summary, the classical C-ALM subproblem employs a greedy ESP solver with λ-guided costs to generate feasible routes that progressively satisfy visit constraints across iterations.

3.3 Multiplier and Penalty Parameter Updates

After each iteration t, once the candidate solution $S^{(t)}$ is obtained, we update the dual multipliers and penalties based on the observed constraint violations.

For each customer-visit constraint,

$$\lambda_j^{(t+1)} = \lambda_j^{(t)} + \rho_j^{(t)}(v_j(S^{(t)}) - 1),$$

where λ_j increases with the magnitude of the violation. For each route R_k, capacity overloads $h_k(S^{(t)}) = \max(0, L(R_k^{(t)}) - Q)$ update the corresponding multiplier as

$$\mu_k^{(t+1)} = \mu_k^{(t)} + \sigma_k^{(t)} h_k(S^{(t)}).$$

Penalty parameters grow only when violations persist:

$$\rho_j^{(t+1)} = \rho_j^{(t)} \times f_\rho, \quad \sigma_k^{(t+1)} = \sigma_k^{(t)} \times f_\sigma,$$

whenever $|v_j(S^{(t)}) - 1| > \varepsilon_{\mathrm{visit}}$ or $h_k(S^{(t)}) > \varepsilon_{\mathrm{cap}}$; otherwise they remain unchanged. Upper bounds $\rho_{\max}$ and $\sigma_{\max}$ cap penalty growth.

This adaptive rule increases dual pressure on recurring violations while stabilizing satisfied constraints, ensuring that feasibility improves steadily without excessive penalty inflation.

3.4 C-ALM Procedure and Convergence

C-ALM integrates the elements described above—route construction, multiplier updates, and penalty adaptation—into a single iterative process. Starting from initialized multipliers and penalty parameters, the algorithm alternates between generating routes via the ESP-based subproblem solver, evaluating constraint violations, and updating dual and penalty terms until convergence.

C-ALM terminates when either a feasible solution is found or the iteration budget is exhausted. Feasibility is declared once both the customer-visit and capacity constraints fall within their respective tolerances:

$$\max_{j} |v_j(S^{(t)}) - 1| \leq \varepsilon_{\text{visit}}, \qquad \max_{k} h_k(S^{(t)}) \leq \varepsilon_{\text{cap}}.$$

If these conditions are not satisfied, the algorithm continues updating multipliers and penalties until the maximum number of iterations $T_{\max}$ is reached.

This tolerance-based convergence criterion allows graceful termination in near-feasible regimes, which is especially important when subproblems are solved heuristically or on noisy quantum backends. In practice, the C-ALM loop balances solution quality, constraint satisfaction, and runtime efficiency, serving as the classical baseline for the hybrid RL- and quantum-enhanced variants presented later.

4 Quantum-Enhanced Augmented Lagrangian Methods

This section introduces the integration of quantum computing into the ALM framework. Two variants are presented: a baseline Quantum-Enhanced ALM (Q-ALM) and a fully integrated RL-guided version (RL-Q-ALM).

4.1 Quantum-Enhanced ALM (Q-ALM)

Q-ALM extends the classical Augmented Lagrangian Method by replacing the route-generation step of C-ALM with a quantum subproblem solver, while retaining the same outer penalty-update loop. At each iteration, a small routing subproblem is encoded as a Quadratic Unconstrained Binary Optimization (QUBO), whose objective combines the original travel costs and the current dual terms:

$$\min_{x} \ x^{\top} Q x = C(x) + \sum_{v} \lambda_v^{(t)} g_v(x),$$

so that quantum optimization is guided by the same multiplier information as in the classical solver.

Quantum Solver. The outer ALM loop iteratively updates routes and multipliers. In each iteration, a small customer subset $S_{\text{sub}} \subseteq C$ is selected, and its local routing subproblem is encoded as a TSP-QUBO (see [10]). The QUBO objective combines travel costs and current dual terms from λ^t, then is mapped to an Ising Hamiltonian and solved by a shallow VQE circuit. The lowest-energy bitstring is decoded into a route, and these partial routes collectively form the candidate solution for that iteration.

Constraint Handling. Subtour elimination and assignment consistency are enforced through standard one-hot permutation constraints included in the QUBO. Penalty magnitudes are automatically scaled by the quantum framework (e.g., Qiskit [42]) to exceed all cost terms, ensuring that infeasible subtours are energetically disfavored.

By substituting only the subproblem solver with a quantum routine, Q-ALM provides a direct comparison baseline to assess how quantum sampling influences route quality and convergence within the ALM framework.

4.2   RL-Guided Quantum-Enhanced ALM (RL-Q-ALM)

Reinforcement Learning-guided Q-ALM (RL-Q-ALM) extends the framework by using deep reinforcement learning to automatically set penalty parameters, the most sensitive component of C-ALM. Instead of heuristic updates, an RL policy predicts optimal initialization values, enabling faster convergence and improved solution quality across diverse CVRP instances.

4.3   Motivation: The Case for Adaptive Penalty Optimization

While the Augmented Lagrangian Method (ALM) effectively enforces CVRP constraints through dual variables λ_j, μ_k and penalties ρ_j, σ_k, its performance depends heavily on how these penalty parameters are chosen. Static or heuristic schedules often require manual tuning and fail to generalize across instances of different sizes and structures [35,37].

To address this, we train a reinforcement learning (RL) agent to predict instance-specific initial penalties $(\rho^{\mathrm{RL}}, \sigma^{\mathrm{RL}})$, providing adaptive initialization for the ALM loop. These learned penalties replace hand-tuned values and remain fixed during optimization $(f_\rho = f_\sigma = 1)$, while multipliers λ_j and μ_k continue to evolve normally. This adaptive initialization enables faster convergence and greater robustness across heterogeneous CVRP instances.

4.4   MDP Formulation

We model the learning task as a single-step Markov Decision Process (MDP) $(\mathcal{S}, \mathcal{A}, R)$, where each CVRP instance constitutes one episode.

State. Each state $s \in \mathbb{R}^6$ encodes instance-level features such as number of customers, vehicle capacity, mean and standard deviation of demands, total demand, and demand-to-capacity ratio:

$$s = [N_c, \, Q, \, \bar{d}, \, \mathrm{std}(d_i), \, D_{\mathrm{total}}, \, D_{\mathrm{total}}/(QN_c)].$$

Action. The agent outputs a continuous pair of penalty parameters:

$$a = (\rho_{\mathrm{pred}}, \sigma_{\mathrm{pred}}), \qquad \rho_{\mathrm{pred}}, \sigma_{\mathrm{pred}} \in \mathbb{R}_+,$$

which initialize the ALM penalties for customer-visit and capacity constraints, respectively.

Reward. After running ALM with the chosen penalties, the agent receives a scalar reward:

$$r = \alpha_1\, R_{\mathrm{BKS}} + \alpha_2\, R_{\mathrm{improve}} - \alpha_3\, I_{\mathrm{ALM}},$$

where R_{BKS} measures cost improvement relative to the Best Known Solution (BKS), R_{improve} rewards self-improvement over the agent's previous best, and the final term penalizes long ALM runs (I_{ALM} iterations). Infeasible solutions yield a large fixed penalty $r = R_{\mathrm{infeasible}} \ll 0$.

This formulation encourages the agent to propose penalty values that produce feasible, high-quality solutions close to the BKS while converging in fewer iterations.

4.5   Learning with Soft Actor–Critic (SAC)

We employ the Soft Actor–Critic (SAC) algorithm [8] to train a policy that maps instance features to optimal penalty parameters. SAC is a model-free, off-policy reinforcement learning method for continuous action spaces, maximizing both expected reward and policy entropy:

$$J(\pi) = \mathbb{E}_{(s,a)\sim\mathcal{D}}[r(s,a) + \alpha\, \mathcal{H}(\pi(\cdot \mid s))],$$

where $\mathcal{D}$ denotes a replay buffer and α controls the trade-off between exploitation and exploration. Actor–critic updates and entropy temperature adaptation follow the standard SAC formulation.

The trained policy $\pi_\phi(s)$ outputs continuous actions

$$a = (\rho_{\mathrm{pred}},\ \sigma_{\mathrm{pred}}),$$

which specify the initial penalty coefficients for the Augmented Lagrangian Method (ALM). During training, the agent learns to propose values that yield feasible, high-quality CVRP solutions with fewer ALM iterations.

4.6   Integration Into the Q-ALM Framework

The learned SAC policy π_ϕ is queried once per CVRP instance to generate penalty initialization values. These actions $a = [\rho_{\mathrm{pred}}, \sigma_{\mathrm{pred}}]$ are integrated into ALM as follows:

1. **Penalty Initialization:**

$$\rho_j^{(0)} \leftarrow \rho_{\mathrm{pred}}, \quad \sigma_k^{(0)} \leftarrow \sigma_{\mathrm{pred}} \quad \forall j \in C,\ \forall k \in \{1,\ldots,K_{\max}\}.$$

2. **Fixed Penalties:**

$$f_\rho = f_\sigma = 1.0 \quad \Rightarrow \quad \rho_j^{(t+1)} = \rho_j^{(t)}, \quad \sigma_k^{(t+1)} = \sigma_k^{(t)}.$$

3. **Lagrange Multiplier Updates:** The multipliers $\lambda_j^{(t)}$ and $\mu_k^{(t)}$ continue to update at each ALM iteration.

This integration produces a hybrid solver, **RL-Q-ALM**, in which the RL policy provides intelligent, instance-specific penalty initialization, and Q-ALM subsequently executes optimization. Unlike classical C-ALM and Q-ALM, where penalties evolve through internal feedback, RL-Q-ALM externalizes this decision, front-loading it into a learned initialization step. Empirically, this decoupling accelerates convergence and improves feasibility consistency across diverse CVRP instances, demonstrating that the agent learns a transferable and effective strategy for solver configuration.

RL-Q-ALM uses the SAC agent to select penalty coefficients, executes a quantum-assisted ALM with VQE-based subproblem solvers, and back-propagates performance feedback to refine the policy. This architecture isolates the benefit of quantum subproblem solving while preserving the same reinforcement learning structure used in the classical counterpart.

Learning Objective and Environment Design. The goal is to train a policy $\pi_\phi(a_t \mid s_t)$ that maps CVRP instance features $s_t \in \mathbb{R}^6$ to penalty parameters $a_t = (\rho_{\text{init}}, \sigma_{\text{init}})$, which initialize the Augmented Lagrangian Method (ALM). These parameters determine the convergence rate, feasibility, and quality of the final solution.

Unlike conventional deterministic solvers, our environment integrates a quantum backend: each ALM subproblem is solved as a QUBO using the Variational Quantum Eigensolver (VQE). Although simulated noiselessly, VQE optimization is non-convex and sensitive to initialization, making the reward landscape highly irregular.

Training is therefore computationally demanding, as each RL episode requires a full ALM run with quantum subproblems. Despite this, the agent must learn efficiently from sparse feedback and generalize across CVRP instances of varying scale and demand patterns.

We design a compact Gym-style environment that encodes CVRP statistics into fixed-length features, interfaces directly with the quantum-enhanced ALM solver, and returns scalar rewards combining feasibility, optimality gap, and convergence cost[1].

5   Empirical Evaluation

This section presents a comparative empirical analysis of our solver paradigms for the CVRP. The evaluation spans two classes of CVRP instances to capture a range of practical and quantum-relevant complexities: (1) small custom-generated instances suitable for QUBO encoding and quantum simulation, and

---

[1] Ayanzadeh et al. [9] explored reinforcement quantum annealing for tuning QUBO penalties on D-Wave hardware; unlike their direct annealing approach, RL-Q-ALM couples learned global penalty initialization with a classical ALM framework and VQE subproblem solver, improving structure and scalability.

(2) real-world benchmark instances from CVRPLIB for compatibility and reproducibility.

Key metrics include:

- **Total Route Cost:** Sum of edge weights across all routes.
- **Optimality Gap:** Deviation from the Best Known Solution (BKS), when available.
- **Feasibility:** Percentage of instances where all ALM constraints are satisfied.
- **Convergence Behavior:** Runtime.

Our findings demonstrate that RL-based tuning improves ALM convergence and feasibility in quantum settings, and that QUBO-based subproblem solving via VQE is feasible for small-scale CVRP instances under simulation.

5.1   Benchmark Instance Classes

To evaluate scalability and generalization, we use two categories of CVRP instances:

(i) Small Synthetic Instances. About 50 problems with $N_c = 5$–8 customers, fixed vehicle capacity $Q = 200$, and random demands in $[10, 40]$. These are used for testing the solver variants, including quantum runs where subproblems can be fully encoded as QUBOs and simulated via VQE.

(ii) Standard CVRPLIB Benchmarks. Seven well-known instances from CVRPLIB [23] (e.g., E-n22-k4, A-n32-k5). These benchmark tests compare classical solvers against best-known solutions, measure optimality gaps, and assess real-world relevance.

6   Experimental Results

We compare four solver variants: **C-ALM**: a classical Augmented Lagrangian Method with heuristic penalty updates; **VQE**: a direct quantum baseline that solves the slack-based QUBO formulation of CVRP, where inequality constraints are converted into equality constraints using slack variables, significantly increasing the number of required qubits; **Q-ALM**: a quantum-augmented ALM that embeds VQE as a subproblem solver within the classical optimization loop; and **RL-Q-ALM**: a hybrid framework in which a reinforcement learning agent adaptively initializes ALM penalties before quantum optimization.

Experiments were conducted on small synthetic CVRP instances, measuring feasibility, optimality, and runtime (Table 1).

Quantum subproblems were solved using the VQE with an `EfficientSU2` ansatz from Qiskit [42]. To mitigate overparameterization and barren plateaus, we employ a single-layer ansatz (`reps=1`), ensuring shallow, trainable circuits suitable for near-term quantum devices.

Table 1. Aggregate performance on *light* (50 instances, $N_c \in [5,8]$) CVRP datasets. Feasibility: percentage of instances where a feasible solution was found. Optimality: percentage of instances solved to the best-known or global optimal.

Instance Set	C-ALM			VQE			Q-ALM			RL-Q-ALM		
	Feas. (%)	Opt. (%)	Time (s)	Feas. (%)	Opt. (%)	Time (s)	Feas. (%)	Opt. (%)	Time (s)	Feas. (%)	Opt. (%)	Time (s)
light	100.0	98.0	0.84	88.0	54.0	232.0	100.0	92.0	211.2	100.0	98.0	166.8

6.1 Aggregate Results on Small Instances

Small Instances $(N_c \in [5,8])$**.** All methods achieved full feasibility. C-ALM was fastest (sub-second runtime), while quantum solvers were slower due to VQE overhead (Q-ALM: 211 s; RL-Q-ALM: 167 s). RL-Q-ALM matched classical optimality (98 %) and improved over plain Q-ALM (92 %), showing that RL initialization enhances quantum solver stability and convergence.

Overall Trends.

– The standalone VQE baseline achieved moderate feasibility (88%) and optimality (54%), demonstrating that quantum optimization alone can find reasonable but suboptimal solutions.
– Integrating VQE within the ALM framework (Q-ALM) substantially improved both solution quality and stability, while RL tuning further enhanced convergence speed and consistency.
– Quantum solvers remain accurate on small problems but are still constrained by execution cost.
– These results highlight the promise of RL-guided quantum optimization as scalable QUBO encodings and quantum hardware continue to advance.

6.2 Detailed Benchmark Performance

In the following we evaluate C-ALM, Q-ALM, and RL-Q-ALM on standard CVRPLIB benchmarks. Table 2 reports optimality gaps (relative to Best Known Solutions) and runtimes, while Fig. 1 visualizes representative solutions on a particular instance A-n32-k5. Note that the standalone VQE evaluation was not performed in these experiments, as directly encoding the full CVRP into a QUBO without the ALM decomposition would require qubit counts far exceeding current simulation run time limits. Our results show that RL-Q-ALM consistently improves upon Q-ALM by producing more compact and feasible routes despite quantum circuit depth and qubit constraints.

Classical vs. Quantum Solvers. C-ALM remains the most reliable baseline, delivering high feasibility and strong optimality across all tested instances. Quantum-augmented variants, while conceptually promising, achieved weaker overall performance but demonstrated measurable benefits from reinforcement learning–based initialization. For example, RL-Q-ALM reduced Q-ALM's optimality gaps

Table 2. Optimality gap (%) and runtime (s) for each method across instances.

Instance	C-ALM		Q-ALM		RL-Q-ALM	
	Gap (%)	Time (s)	Gap (%)	Time (s)	Gap (%)	Time (s)
E-n13-k4	0.00	7.48	14.17	3354.73	4.04	2875.63
E-n22-k4	4.53	435.96	22.93	9216.58	20.53	8152.59
E-n23-k3	0.00	1041.59	9.66	9955.44	10.54	8710.78
E-n30-k3	7.86	2136.31	17.60	11835.36	14.23	10460.11
E-n31-k7	8.70	6980.96	20.31	13914.72	19.26	12215.95
B-n31-k5	4.01	2582.80	17.11	12830.76	19.64	11244.06
A-n32-k5	17.09	10913.16	19.64	16873.20	18.36	14891.41

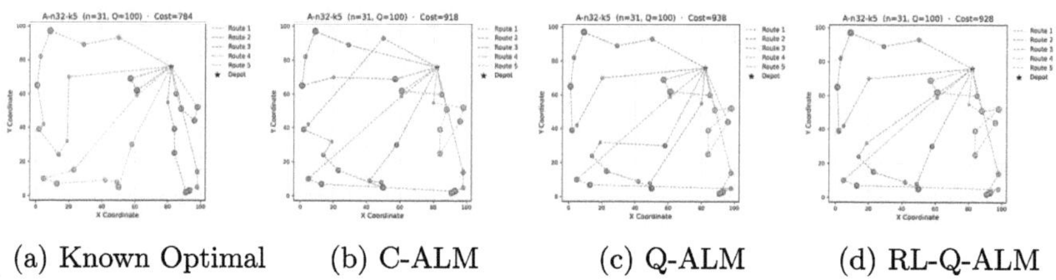

(a) Known Optimal   (b) C-ALM   (c) Q-ALM   (d) RL-Q-ALM

Fig. 1. Comparison of route structures for instance A-n32-k5 across ALM variants.

by 3–10% on solvable cases (E-n13-k4: 14.2% → 4.0%; E-n30-k3: 17.6% → 14.2%), showing that adaptive penalty learning can improve quantum solver stability and convergence.

Runtime Overhead. Quantum execution remained 10×–100× slower than classical optimization due to repeated QUBO construction, VQE circuit evaluation, and bitstring decoding. For instance, E-n13-k4 required 7.5 s with C-ALM versus over 3350 s with Q-ALM. Even under noiseless simulation, these overheads dominate total runtime, underscoring current scalability limitations of quantum approaches.

6.3 Overall Summary of Findings

Synthesizing the results from Tables 1 and 2, the key conclusions are:

- **Reinforcement learning enhances ALM performance**, RL-Q-ALM demonstrates that intelligent parameter initialization can partially offset the instability and non-convexity inherent to quantum variational optimization, yielding better-quality solutions without altering the underlying ALM structure.
- **Quantum-augmented solvers (Q-ALM and RL-Q-ALM)** are effective primarily on small CVRP instances ($N_c \leq 8$). RL-Q-ALM outperforms Q-

ALM in both optimality and convergence consistency, but remains below classical results overall.

- **Scalability and runtime challenges** persist for quantum methods, with VQE execution times 10^1–$10^2\times$ slower than classical ALM due to circuit depth, iterative optimization, and bitstring decoding overheads.
- **Outlook:** Classical ALM remains the most practical near-term approach, while RL-guided quantum optimization represents a forward-looking path toward adaptive, hybrid solvers that could benefit from advances in hardware, encoding efficiency, and error mitigation.

7   Future Research Directions

Future work will advance along three directions. **(i) Hardware scalability and encoding:** extend the framework to real quantum devices using error mitigation, hardware-efficient ansätze, and compact, symmetry-aware QUBO encodings that embed routing constraints. **(ii) RL generalization:** improve transferability through meta-learning and graph-based representations, and refine multi-objective rewards balancing cost, feasibility, and runtime. **(iii) Hybrid integration and theory:** integrate quantum subroutines into adaptive RL-guided pipelines and develop theoretical analyses of convergence and stability under noisy conditions. Together, these efforts aim to transition RL-Quantum optimization from simulation to scalable, hardware-relevant applications in logistics and beyond.

References

1. Dantzig, G.B., Ramser, J.H.: The truck dispatching problem. Manage. Sci. **6**(1), 80–91 (1959)
2. Clarke, G., Wright, J.W.: Scheduling of vehicles from a central depot to a number of delivery points. Oper. Res. **12**(4), 568–581 (1964)
3. Birgin, E.G., Martínez, J.M.: Practical Augmented Lagrangian Methods for Constrained Optimization. SIAM, Philadelphia (2014)
4. Hestenes, M.R.: Multiplier and gradient methods. J. Optim. Theory Appl. **4**(5), 303–320 (1969). https://doi.org/10.1007/BF00927673
5. Powell, M.J.D.: A method for nonlinear constraints in minimization problems. In: Fletcher, R. (ed.) Optimization, pp. 283–298. Academic Press, New York (1969)
6. Held, M., Karp, R.M.: The traveling-salesman problem and minimum spanning trees: Part II. Math. Program. **1**(1), 6–25 (1971)
7. Fisher, M.L.: The Lagrangian relaxation method for solving integer programming problems. Manage. Sci. **27**(1), 1–18 (1981)
8. Graf, P., Annoni, J., Bay, C., Lunacek, D.W., Jones, W.E.: Distributed reinforcement learning with ADMM-RL. In: Proceedings of American Control Conference (ACC), pp. 4159–4166 (2019)
9. Ayanzadeh, R., Halem, M., Finin, T.: Reinforcement quantum annealing: a hybrid quantum learning automata. Sci. Rep. **10**, 7952 (2020)
10. Lucas, A.: Ising formulations of many NP problems. Front. Phys. **2**, 5 (2014)

11. Toth, P., Vigo, D.: The Vehicle Routing Problem. SIAM, Philadelphia (2002)
12. Peruzzo, A., et al.: A variational eigenvalue solver on a photonic quantum processor. Nat. Commun. **5**(1), 4213 (2014)
13. Liao, F.-Y., Zheng, Y.: A bundle-based augmented Lagrangian framework: algorithm, convergence, and primal-dual principles. arXiv preprint arXiv:2502.08835 (2025). https://arxiv.org/abs/2502.08835
14. Bai, X., Sun, J., Zheng, X.: An augmented Lagrangian decomposition method for chance-constrained optimization problems. INFORMS J. Comput. (2020)
15. Song, M., Cheng, L., Lu, B.: Solving the multi-compartment vehicle routing problem by an augmented Lagrangian relaxation method. Expert Syst. Appl. **237**, 121511 (2024). https://doi.org/10.1016/j.eswa.2023.121511. https://www.sciencedirect.com/science/article/pii/S0957417423020134
16. Song, M., Cheng, L.: An augmented Lagrangian relaxation method for the mean-standard deviation based vehicle routing problem. Knowl. Based Syst. **247**, 108736 (2022). https://doi.org/10.1016/j.knosys.2022.108736. https://www.sciencedirect.com/science/article/pii/S0950705122003458
17. Lenstra, J.K., Rinnooy Kan, A.H.G.: Complexity of vehicle routing and scheduling problems. Networks, **11**(2), 221–227 (1981)
18. Lysgaard, J., Letchford, A.N., Eglese, R.W.: A new branch-and-cut algorithm for the capacitated vehicle routing problem. Math. Program. **100**, 423–445 (2004)
19. Gendreau, M., Hertz, A., Laporte, G.: A tabu search heuristic for the vehicle routing problem. Manage. Sci. **40**(10), 1276–1290 (1994)
20. Laporte, G., Semet, F.: Classical heuristics for the capacitated VRP. In: The Vehicle Routing Problem, pp. 109–128. SIAM (2002)
21. Nazari, M., Oroojlooy, A., Snyder, L., Takác, M.: Reinforcement learning for solving the vehicle routing problem. NeurIPS**31** (2018)
22. Fitzek, D., Ghandriz, T., Laine, L., Granath, M., Kockum, A.F.: Applying quantum approximate optimization to the heterogeneous vehicle routing problem. Sci. Rep. **14**(1), 25415 (2024)
23. Uchoa, E., et al.: New benchmark instances for the capacitated vehicle routing problem. Eur. J. Oper. Res. **257**(3), 845–858 (2017)
24. Sharma, M., Lau, H.C.: Cutting Slack: Quantum optimization with slack-free methods for combinatorial benchmarks. arXiv:2507.12159 (2025)
25. Sharma, M., Lau, H.C.: A comparative study of quantum optimization techniques for solving combinatorial optimization benchmark problems. arXiv:2503.12121 (2025)
26. Boyd, S., Parikh, N., Chu, E., Peleato, B., Eckstein, J.: Distributed optimization and statistical learning via the alternating direction method of multipliers. Found. Trends Mach. Learn. **3**(1), 1–122 (2011)
27. Feillet, D., Dejax, P., Gendreau, M., Gueguen, C.: An exact algorithm for the elementary shortest path problem with resource constraints: Application to some vehicle routing problems. Netw. Int. J. **44**(3), 216–229 (2004)
28. Lozano, L., Duque, D., Medaglia, A.L.: An exact algorithm for the elementary shortest path problem with resource constraints. Transp. Sci. **50**(1), 348–357 (2016)
29. Righini, G., Salani, M.: Symmetry helps: bounded bi-directional dynamic programming for the elementary shortest path problem with resource constraints. Discret. Optim. **3**(3), 255–273 (2006)
30. Wright, S., Nocedal, J.: Numerical Optimization, vol. 35, no. 67–68, p. 7. Springer, Cham (1999)

31. Stooke, A., Achiam, J., Abbeel, P.: Responsive safety in reinforcement learning by PID Lagrangian methods. In: Proceedings of the International Conference on Machine Learning, pp. 9133–9143. PMLR (2020)
32. Fisher, M.L., Jaikumar, R.: A generalized assignment heuristic for vehicle routing. Networks **11**(2), 109–124 (1981)
33. Kallehauge, B., Larsen, J., Madsen, O.B.G.: Lagrangian duality applied to the vehicle routing problem with time windows. Comput. Oper. Res. **33**(5), 1464–1487 (2006)
34. Toth, P., Vigo, D.: Vehicle Routing: Problems, Methods, and Applications. SIAM, Philadelphia (2014)
35. Bollapragada, R., Karamanli, C., Keith, B., Lazarov, B., Petrides, S., Wang, J.: An adaptive sampling augmented Lagrangian method for stochastic optimization with deterministic constraints. Comput. Math. Appl. **149**, 239–258 (2023)
36. Zhang, T., et al.: Predictive Lagrangian optimization for constrained reinforcement learning. arXiv preprint arXiv:2501.15217 (2025)
37. Xiao, N., Liu, X., Yuan, Y.-X.: A class of smooth exact penalty function methods for optimization problems with orthogonality constraints. Optim. Methods Softw. **37**(4), 1205–1241 (2022)
38. Zeng, S., Kody, A., Kim, Y., Kim, K., Molzahn, D.K.: A reinforcement learning approach to parameter selection for distributed optimal power flow. Electr. Power Syst. Res. **212**, 108546 (2022)
39. Li, J., Fridovich-Keil, D., Sojoudi, S., Tomlin, C.J.: Augmented Lagrangian method for instantaneously constrained reinforcement learning problems. In: Proceedings of the 60th IEEE Conference on Decision and Control (CDC), pp. 2982–2989. IEEE (2021)
40. Chen, S., Yu, H., Yagoobi, J., Shao, C.: Reinforcement learning constrained beam search for parameter optimization of paper drying under flexible constraints. arXiv preprint arXiv:2501.12542 (2025). https://arxiv.org/abs/2501.12542
41. Ji, T., Luo, Y., Sun, F., Jing, M., He, F., Huang, W.: When to update your model: constrained model-based reinforcement learning. arXiv preprint arXiv:2210.08349 (2023). https://arxiv.org/abs/2210.08349
42. Javadi-Abhari, A., et al.: Quantum computing with Qiskit. arXiv preprint arXiv:2405.08810 (2024). https://arxiv.org/abs/2405.08810

Learning-Based Graph Shrinking
for Quantum Optimization of Constrained
Combinatorial Problems

Monit Sharma[ID] and Hoong Chuin Lau[(✉)][ID]

School of Computing and Information Systems Singapore Management University,
Singapore, Singapore
{monitsharma,hclau}@smu.edu.sg

Abstract. Graph shrinking has recently emerged as a powerful preprocessing technique for hybrid classical–quantum optimization, enabling variable and constraint reduction before quantum solving. Conventional approaches rely on Semi-Definite Programming (SDP) relaxations to compute vertex correlations, but these methods suffer from high computational overhead, instance-specific tuning, and limited generalizability. In this work, we replace the handcrafted SDP correlation stage with a reinforcement learning (RL) based correlation estimator, trained to predict merge quality directly from graph structure. We reformulate the graph shrinking process as a Markov Decision Process (MDP), design a Graph Neural Network (GNN) policy to guide vertex merging, and integrate the learned correlations into a hybrid classical–quantum pipeline. Experiments on benchmark problems, including the Maximum Independent Set (MIS) and Multi-Dimensional Knapsack Problem (MDKP), demonstrate that our Learned Graph Shrinking (LGS) achieves comparable or superior solution quality to SDP-guided and random baselines, while reducing qubit requirements by up to 35%. These results highlight the potential of learning-based correlation estimation as a scalable and general alternative to classical relaxations for quantum optimization.

Keywords: Graph Shrinking · Reinforcement Learning · Quantum Optimization · Variational Quantum Eigensolver · QUBO · Hybrid Quantum-Classical Computing

1 Introduction

Combinatorial Optimization Problems (COPs) are central to domains such as logistics [1], finance [2], and machine learning [3], yet remain NP-hard and challenging to scale. Among them, the weighted Max-Cut problem exemplifies this difficulty [29]. Quantum algorithms such as QAOA [20] and VQE [21] show promise for QUBO formulations, yet current hardware, for example IBM Osprey (433 q) [31], IBM Condor (1,121 q) [30], Fujitsu–RIKEN (256 q) [32], and Quantinuum Helios (98 q) [33], still constrains problem size and connectivity.

A promising remedy is *graph shrinking* [28] reducing problem size by merging highly correlated vertices derived from Semi-Definite Programming (SDP) relaxations. However, this handcrafted correlation estimation presents key drawbacks: (i) high computational overhead due to repeated SDP solves, (ii) static, instance-specific correlations that fail to adapt across iterations, and (iii) poor generalization across different problem families (e.g., MIS, MDKP, etc.). These limitations motivate a shift toward *learning-based correlation estimation* that is adaptive, transferable, and computationally efficient.

We propose a reinforcement learning (RL) framework that replaces static SDP correlations with a *learned adaptive correlation policy*. By reformulating graph shrinking as a Markov Decision Process (MDP), our method learns to merge vertices sequentially using feedback from reduction quality and structural preservation. A Graph Neural Network (GNN) policy encodes node features and graph structure, enabling the model to generalize across instance scales and problem types. The learned correlations integrate seamlessly into hybrid classicalquantum pipelines, yielding reduced problem instances compatible with QAOA and VQE solvers.

Our main contributions are:

1. We reformulate graph shrinking as an **MDP** for adaptive correlation learning.
2. We design a **GNN-based policy** that guides vertex merging dynamically.
3. We integrate the learned correlations into **hybrid classicalquantum optimization pipelines**.
4. Experimentally, we demonstrate scalability and performance improvement in two classical combinatorial optimization problems **MIS**, and **MDKP** on benchmark instances [26,27].

In summary, this work bridges handcrafted correlation heuristics and data-driven adaptation, establishing a general, scalable framework for learning correlation structures in hybrid quantum optimization.

2   Background and Motivation

In our preliminary work [28], *Adaptive Graph Shrinking* (AGS) was introduced as a preprocessing technique to reduce the dimensionality of combinatorial optimization problems before quantum solving. The method computes a correlation matrix X_{SDP} from a Semi-Definite Programming (SDP) relaxation of the weighted Max-Cut formulation, where each entry X_{ij} reflects the alignment between nodes i and j. Vertices with strong correlations $|X_{ij}| \approx 1$ are iteratively merged, producing a smaller graph that preserves the structural essence of the original problem [22,23]. This correlation-driven contraction has proven effective in compressing large-scale instances while maintaining feasibility in downstream quantum optimization [22,23,28].

Limitations of the SDP-Based Process. Despite its success, SDP-based correlation estimation remains computationally demanding and inherently *instance-specific*. Solving the SDP relaxation becomes prohibitive for graphs beyond a few hundred nodes. Moreover, X_{SDP} depends on a single static snapshot of the problem, any structural change during iterative shrinking invalidates it, requiring full recomputation. Finally, correlations learned for one instance do not generalize to others, restricting scalability across problem classes such as MIS, MDKP, etc.

Learning-Based Correlation Prediction. To overcome these limitations, we propose in this paper an RL approach that replaces handcrafted SDP correlations with a *learned correlation estimator* parameterized by θ, such that:

$$X_{\text{RL}} \approx f_\theta(G),$$

where f_θ maps graph features to pairwise correlation estimates [9,10]. The RL model learns to approximate the functional behavior of the SDP solver while adapting to evolving graph structures during the shrinking process. This allows the graph shrinking algorithm to make near real-time merge decisions without repeatedly solving SDP relaxations.

Implication. By learning correlations directly from structural and spectral graph features [12], f_θ generalizes across instances and problem types, drastically reducing preprocessing cost and enabling fully adaptive, end-to-end graph shrinking for hybrid classicalquantum optimization.

3   Problem Formulation

We formalize the process of iterative graph shrinking as a *Markov Decision Process (MDP)* defined by the tuple $(\mathcal{S}, \mathcal{A}, P, R, \gamma)$ [8]. The agent sequentially merges correlated vertices while maintaining structural feasibility and optimization quality. The objective is to learn a policy $\pi(a \mid s)$ that maximizes the expected cumulative discounted reward:

$$\mathbb{E}_\pi\left[\sum_{t=0}^{T} \gamma^t R(s_t, a_t)\right].$$

3.1   State Space $\mathcal{S}$

At time step t, the state $s_t \in \mathcal{S}$ encodes the current supernode graph:

$$G_t = (V_t, E_t, F_t),$$

where V_t is the set of current supernodes, E_t the induced edges among them, and $F_t \in \mathbb{R}^{|V_t| \times d}$ a feature matrix describing each supernode (e.g., size, average degree, internal density, and correlation statistics). Initially, each vertex forms a singleton supernode, $V_0 = \{\{v_1\}, \ldots, \{v_n\}\}$, and features are derived from the original graph.

3.2   Action Space $\mathcal{A}$

An action $a_t \in \mathcal{A}(s_t)$ corresponds to selecting a pair of distinct supernodes to merge:

$$a_t = (C_u, C_v), \quad C_u, C_v \in V_t, \ C_u \neq C_v.$$

The action space is dynamic, with $\binom{|V_t|}{2}$ possible merges at step t. Each action represents a potential contraction guided by the learned correlation estimator $f_\theta(G_t)$.

3.3   Transition Function P

The transition function $P(s_{t+1} \mid s_t, a_t)$ is deterministic. Executing $a_t = (C_u, C_v)$ produces a new state s_{t+1} by:

$$V_{t+1} = (V_t \backslash \{C_u, C_v\}) \cup \{C_u \cup C_v\},$$
$$E_{t+1} = \text{update edges based on original connectivity},$$
$$F_{t+1} = \text{recompute supernode features}.$$

Thus, $P(s_{t+1} \mid s_t, a_t) = 1$, and the order of merging (C_u, C_v) is irrelevant.

3.4   Reward Function R

The reward function balances local feasibility with global objective preservation:

$$R(s_t, a_t) = R_{\text{intermediate}}(s_t, a_t) + R_{\text{terminal}}(s_T).$$

Intermediate Reward:

$$R_{\text{intermediate}}(s_t, a_t) = \begin{cases} +1, & \text{if merged supernode is feasible,} \\ -2, & \text{if feasibility constraints are violated.} \end{cases}$$

Feasibility depends on the target problem (e.g., adjacency in MIS, capacity in MDKP, etc.).

Terminal Reward: Once the episode terminates (after reaching the target node count k or a spectral threshold $\lambda_{\min}$), a composite score measures compression quality:

$$R_{\text{terminal}} = w_f(1 - \text{gap}_{\text{final}}) + w_r Q_{\text{recon}} + w_s S_{\text{spec}},$$

where $\text{gap}_{\text{final}}$ quantifies deviation from optimal cost after reconstruction, Q_{recon} measures recoverability of the original structure, and S_{spec} penalizes excessive loss of spectral information. We use weights w_f, w_r, w_s to balance these objectives.

3.5   Discount Factor γ

The discount factor $\gamma \in [0, 1]$ governs the agent's planning horizon. Higher γ (e.g., 0.99) encourages long-term shrink quality, prioritizing stable and globally consistent merges over myopic decisions.

3.6 Termination Criterion

The shrinking process terminates when either:

1. The number of remaining supernodes $|V_t|$ reaches a predefined target k, or
2. The smallest nonzero Laplacian eigenvalue $\lambda_2(G_t)$ exceeds a spectral threshold, indicating that further merging would distort structural integrity.

This spectral criterion ensures that the reduced graph remains representative of the original topology.

3.7 Composite Objective

The overall goal is to learn a policy π_θ that maximizes the expected discounted sum of rewards, reflecting a trade-off between compression, constraint satisfaction, and recoverability:

$$\pi_\theta^* = \arg\max_{\pi_\theta} \mathbb{E}_{\pi_\theta} \left[\sum_{t=0}^{T} \gamma^t R(s_t, a_t) \right].$$

This MDP formulation transforms graph shrinking into a sequential decision-making problem where the RL agent adaptively learns correlations and merges, achieving real-time scalability without repeated SDP computations.

4 Learning Framework

Building on the MDP formulation, this section presents the learning framework that replaces handcrafted SDP correlations with data-driven estimates [14]. A Graph Neural Network (GNN) policy encodes node and graph features to infer correlation strengths and predict merge actions directly from structure, enabling adaptive and scalable graph shrinking within the hybrid classicalquantum pipeline.

4.1 Graph Representation

Each state s_t in the MDP is represented by a graph $G_t = (V_t, E_t, F_t)$, where both structural and constraint-aware information are embedded as input features to the policy network. The representation unifies three complementary views of the graph: topological connectivity, spectral structure, and constraint information derived from the underlying combinatorial formulation.

Adjacency and Laplacian Encodings. The structural backbone of G_t is defined by the adjacency matrix $A_t \in \mathbb{R}^{|V_t| \times |V_t|}$, where $(A_t)_{ij} = 1$ if an edge exists between supernodes C_i and C_j. Self-loops are added to stabilize message passing, giving $\hat{A}_t = A_t + I$. The normalized graph Laplacian $L_t = I - D_t^{-1/2} \hat{A}_t D_t^{-1/2}$, with degree matrix $D_t = \mathrm{diag}(\sum_j \hat{A}_{t,ij})$, encodes spectral properties that capture global connectivity and community structure. Both $\hat{A}_t$ and L_t are provided to the Graph Neural Network (GNN) layers to enable simultaneous local and spectral reasoning during policy evaluation. Using both adjacency and Laplacian-based (spectral) encodings has been shown effective in capturing both local and global graph structure [15].

Constraint-Aware Node Features. Each supernode $C_i \in V_t$ is associated with a feature vector $f_i \in \mathbb{R}^d$ describing its structural and constraint statistics [16]:

$$f_i = [\, |C_i|, \ \rho_i, \ d_i, \ \phi_i, \ \psi_i \,],$$

where:

- **Supernode size** $|C_i|$: number of original vertices contained in C_i.
- **Internal density** $\rho_i = 2|E(C_i)|/(|C_i|(|C_i|-1))$: measures intra-connectivity within C_i.
- **Degree** $d_i = \sum_j A_{t,ij}$: external connectivity capturing the interaction strength with other supernodes.
- **Constraint penalty** ϕ_i: cumulative violation score of problem-specific feasibility rules (e.g., adjacency conflicts in MIS, capacity overflows in MDKP, or permutation overlap in QAP).
- **Normalized correlation feature** ψ_i: mean pairwise correlation between nodes inside C_i, derived either from X_{SDP} in pretraining or from the learned estimator $f_\theta(G_t)$ during training.

Composite Feature Matrix. Collecting all supernode features yields

$$F_t = [f_1^\top, f_2^\top, \ldots, f_{|V_t|}^\top]^\top \in \mathbb{R}^{|V_t| \times d}$$

The triplet $(\hat{A}_t, L_t, F_t)$ forms the complete input to the GNN encoder within the RL policy. This encoding allows the agent to integrate structural, spectral, and constraint information, enabling informed, near-real-time merge decisions without recomputing costly SDP correlations.

4.2   Policy Network

The policy network approximates the actionvalue function $Q(s, a; \theta)$, where θ denotes all trainable parameters. It consists of two main components: a Graph Neural Network (GNN) encoder [13] that extracts structural and constraint-aware representations from the current graph, and a Multi-Layer Perceptron (MLP) head that predicts the Q-value of potential merge actions [14].

GNN-Based Encoder. At each step t, the current state s_t is represented by a graph $G_t = (V_t, E_t, F_t)$ with adjacency matrix A_t and feature matrix F_t (defined in Sect. 4.1). We employ a Graph Convolutional Network (GCN) to generate latent embeddings for each supernode:

$$H^{(\ell+1)} = \sigma\!\left(\hat{D}^{-1/2}\hat{A}\hat{D}^{-1/2}H^{(\ell)}W^{(\ell)}\right),$$

where $\hat{A} = A_t + I$ adds self-loops, $\hat{D}$ is its degree matrix, $H^{(0)} = F_t$, and $\sigma(\cdot)$ is a non-linear activation (ReLU). After L layers, we obtain $H^{(L)} \in \mathbb{R}^{|V_t| \times k}$, where each row h_v is the embedding of supernode v. This operation aggregates both local topology and global constraint signals, allowing the network to reason over structural similarity and merge feasibility simultaneously.

Q-Value Head. Given a candidate merge action $a_t = (u, v)$, the model concatenates the embeddings of the two selected supernodes and predicts the corresponding Q-value:

$$Q(s_t, a_t; \theta) = f_\theta([h_u \| h_v]),$$

where $[h_u \| h_v] \in \mathbb{R}^{2k}$ denotes concatenation and $f_\theta : \mathbb{R}^{2k} \to \mathbb{R}$ is implemented as a feed-forward MLP with one or more hidden layers. The output scalar approximates the expected discounted return of performing the merge (u, v) in state s_t.

Interpretation. The GNN encoder learns context-dependent embeddings that capture each supernode's structural role and constraint status, while the MLP head evaluates pairwise compatibility for merging [19]. Together, they form an expressive, permutation-invariant architecture that generalizes across varying graph sizes and problem types. This unified network enables the agent to make real-time, data-driven merge decisions without recomputing SDP correlations.

4.3   Training Objective

The policy network is trained via Deep Q-Learning (DQN) [17] to approximate the optimal actionvalue function $Q^*(s, a)$ that maximizes the expected discounted reward of the graph-shrinking MDP. The optimization objective minimizes the Bellman error between the predicted and target Q-values:

$$\mathcal{L}(\theta) = \mathbb{E}_{(s,a,r,s')}\left[\left(r + \gamma \max_{a'} Q(s', a'; \theta^-) - Q(s, a; \theta)\right)^2\right],$$

where θ and θ^- denote the parameters of the main and target networks, respectively. The target network is a delayed copy of the main Q-network, updated every τ steps or via soft updates $\theta^- \leftarrow \tau\theta + (1 - \tau)\theta^-$, ensuring training stability.

Experience Replay. Transitions (s_t, a_t, r_t, s_{t+1}) are stored in a replay buffer $\mathcal{D}$ to decorrelate sequential samples and improve data efficiency [18]. Mini-batches $\{(s_i, a_i, r_i, s'_i)\}_{i=1}^B$ are randomly drawn from $\mathcal{D}$ to compute stochastic gradient updates of $\mathcal{L}(\theta)$ using Adam or SGD optimizers.

Exploration Strategy. To balance exploration and exploitation, the agent follows an ϵ-greedy policy:

$$a_t = \begin{cases} \text{random action from } \mathcal{A}(s_t), & \text{with probability } \epsilon, \\ \arg\max_a Q(s_t, a; \theta), & \text{with probability } 1 - \epsilon. \end{cases}$$

The exploration rate ϵ is annealed from a high initial value (e.g., $\epsilon_0 = 1.0$) to a small minimum (e.g., $\epsilon_{\min} = 0.05$) throughout training, encouraging early exploration and late exploitation.

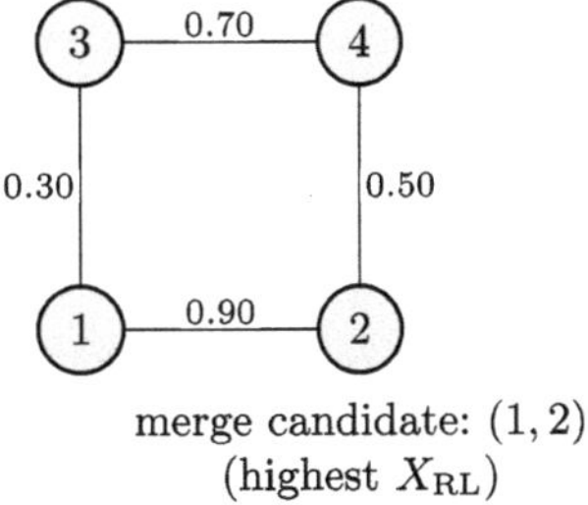

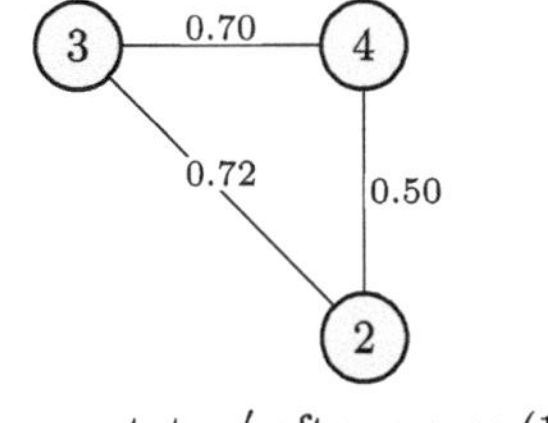

(a) Initial graph with learned correlations $X_{\mathrm{RL}}(i, j) = Q(s, (i, j); \theta)$.

(b) State after executing the best merge $(1, 2)$.

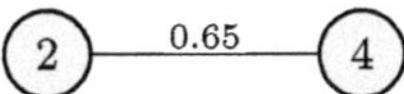

termination (target size / spectral threshold)

(c) Final reduced graph used by the quantum solver.

Fig. 1. Learned Graph Shrinking (LGS) workflow. (a) The process begins with the initial problem graph, where edges are annotated with learned correlations $X_{\mathrm{RL}}(i, j) = Q(s, (i, j); \theta)$ predicted by the policy network. **(b)** The edge with the highest correlation (e.g., $(1, 2)$) is selected, and the corresponding nodes are merged to form a supernode, producing a reduced graph. **(c)** This iterative merging continues until the graph reaches a target size or satisfies a spectral stopping criterion. The final reduced instance is then passed to the downstream QAOA/VQE solver, followed by solution reconstruction and feasibility repair.

Training Dynamics. At each iteration, the Q-network predicts action values for all candidate merges, the chosen action is executed, and the resulting transition is stored in $\mathcal{D}$. Gradients are computed by minimizing $\mathcal{L}(\theta)$, and the network parameters are updated via backpropagation. The combination of experience replay, a target network, and ϵ-greedy exploration stabilizes convergence and prevents oscillations, allowing the learned policy to generalize across graph sizes and problem types.

Figure 1 illustrates the overall workflow of the proposed Learned Graph Shrinking (LGS) method. Starting from an initial problem graph, the RL agent iteratively predicts edge correlations, merges the most promising node pairs, and progressively compresses the instance until a target structural or spectral criterion is satisfied. The resulting reduced graph is then optimized using a downstream quantum solver such as QAOA or VQE.

4.4   Generalization Strategy

In this work, we train *specialist models*, where a separate policy $\pi_\theta^{(p)}$ is optimized for each problem class, namely, the Maximum Independent Set (MIS) and Multi-Dimensional Knapsack Problem (MDKP). This specialization enables the agent to capture domain-specific graph patterns and constraint structures, leading to faster convergence and more stable performance.

While our experiments focus on specialist models, the framework can be extended to a *generalist policy* π_θ^{gen} trained on mixed problem datasets. Such a model could incorporate class identifiers or normalized constraint features to enable cross-domain adaptation, supporting a scalable, problem-agnostic learning approach for future work.

5   Integration with Quantum Optimization

The reinforcement learning (RL) framework naturally integrates into the hybrid classicalquantum optimization pipeline by substituting the computationally intensive SDP correlation stage with a learned estimator. Instead of explicitly solving a Semi-Definite Program to compute the correlation matrix X_{SDP}, we define:

$$X_{\text{RL}}(i,j) = Q(s_t,(i,j);\theta),$$

where $Q(s_t,(i,j);\theta)$ is the Q-value predicted by the policy network for the merge action (i,j) in state s_t. This scalar serves as a *learned correlation strength* reflecting the expected long-term reward of merging supernodes i and j, implicitly capturing structural similarity, constraint feasibility, and compression potential.

Shrinking Phase. The RL-derived correlation matrix X_{RL} guides the merging process exactly as X_{SDP} did in the original Adaptive Graph Shrinking (AGS) [28] pipeline. At each iteration, candidate merges (i,j) with the highest $X_{\text{RL}}(i,j)$ values are executed, progressively reducing the number of nodes while preserving problem structure. Since Q-values are obtained directly from the learned model, this procedure enables near real-time shrinkage without repeated SDP solves.

Spectral Stopping Criterion. The shrinking continues until either the target node count k is reached or the second smallest eigenvalue of the Laplacian, $\lambda_2(G_t)$, exceeds a spectral threshold. This ensures that the reduced graph retains its essential topology and connectivity patterns [4–7].

Solution Reconstruction and Repair. After the shrinking phase, the reduced instance is solved using a downstream quantum optimizer (e.g., QAOA or VQE [20,21]). The obtained solution is then *lifted* back to the original space by expanding merged supernodes. A lightweight feasibility-repair heuristic corrects any residual violations of problem constraints (e.g., overlapping items in MDKP or adjacent selections in MIS).

So, replacing X_{SDP} with the learned $X_{\text{RL}} = Q(s_t,(i,j);\theta)$ enables a fully adaptive, data-driven graph shrinking mechanism that seamlessly integrates into existing classicalquantum workflows.

6 Experimental Setup

6.1 Datasets and Benchmarks

We evaluate the proposed RL-based graph shrinking framework on two well-studied combinatorial optimization problems, Maximum Independent Set (MIS) [27] and Multi-Dimensional Knapsack (MDKP) [26], using the same benchmark instances as in [24,25,28] to ensure reproducibility and consistent comparison.

All datasets are publicly available [11], and the same instances are reused from prior work [28] to ensure direct comparability of results and runtime statistics.

6.2 Graph-Shrinking Methods

We evaluate three graph-shrinking strategies within the hybrid classicalquantum optimization pipeline: the original SDP-based Adaptive Graph Shrinking (AGS) [28], the proposed reinforcement learningbased Learned Graph Shrinking (LGS), and the stochastic Naïve Graph Shrinking (NGS) approach.

- **SDP-Based Shrinking (AGS):** The Adaptive Graph Shrinking (AGS) method [28] computes correlations X_{SDP} via Semi-Definite Programming (SDP) relaxations. These correlations guide vertex merging in descending order of X_{SDP}, followed by spectral stopping and reconstruction. AGS serves as a strong classical reference for correlation-driven graph reduction.
- **RL-Based Shrinking (LGS):** The proposed Learned Graph Shrinking (LGS) replaces the handcrafted SDP correlation matrix X_{SDP} with learned correlations $X_{\mathrm{RL}}(i,j) = Q(s_t, (i,j); \theta)$ predicted by the trained policy network. Merge operations are executed in descending order of X_{RL}, following the same spectral stopping and reconstruction steps as AGS. By learning correlations directly from structural features, LGS achieves adaptive, instance-specific shrinking without solving costly SDP relaxations.
- **Random Merging (NGS):** The Naïve Graph Shrinking (NGS) approach performs random merging, selecting pairs of supernodes uniformly at random until the target node count is reached. This stochastic strategy provides a lower reference for evaluating the benefits of correlation-guided methods such as AGS and LGS.

6.3 Evaluation Metrics

Performance is evaluated using four complementary metrics:

- **Optimality Gap (%):** Relative deviation from the best-known or optimal solution, $\mathrm{Gap} = 100 \times (|f_{\mathrm{final}} - f_{\mathrm{opt}}|/f_{\mathrm{opt}})$.
- **Relative Solution Quality (RSQ %):** The ratio between the final objective value and the best-known value, $\mathrm{RSQ} = 100 \times (f_{\mathrm{final}}/f_{\mathrm{opt}})$.

– **Qubits Used:** The number of qubits required to represent the problem after graph shrinking. This reflects the effective problem size and directly indicates the reduction achieved by each method.

Together, these metrics capture the balance between scalability (qubits used), and optimization quality (optimality gap and RSQ), enabling a consistent evaluation of classical, learning-based, and naïve graph-shrinking strategies.

7 Results and Discussion

7.1 Experimental Results

Tables 1 and 2 present the comparative performance of the proposed Learned Graph Shrinking (LGS) method against the Adaptive Graph Shrinking (AGS) [28] and Naïve Graph Shrinking (NGS) baselines, alongside direct VQE optimization on the *original unshrunk QUBO*. While VQE operates on the full problem graph, AGS, NGS, and LGS are evaluated on shrunk graphs using reduced qubit counts as shown in the tables.

MIS Results. For the Maximum Independent Set benchmarks, the learned policy achieves solution quality comparable to or exceeding SDP-guided AGS while requiring **2035% fewer qubits.** For instance, in `1et.64`, LGS achieves 100% relative solution quality with only 46 qubits, outperforming AGS (88.9%) and VQE (77.8%) on the 64-qubit unshrunk problem. Across all MIS instances, LGS maintains robust performance consistency, demonstrating that the RL-trained correlation model effectively captures structural relationships without reliance on expensive SDP relaxations (Fig. 2).

Table 1. Performance comparison on MIS benchmarks. Values in AGS, NGS, LGS, and VQE columns represent the **Relative Solution Quality (RSQ %)** as defined in Eq. (5), measuring solution quality relative to the best-known optimum. **Qubits (QUBO)** denotes the number of qubits required for the original unshrunk QUBO instance, while **Qubits (Shrink)** corresponds to the reduced qubit count after graph shrinking. **AGS**, **NGS**, and **LGS** correspond to results on *shrunk graphs* produced by Adaptive (SDP-based), Naïve (random), and Learned (RL-based, proposed) graph shrinking, respectively. **VQE** reports RSQ (%) obtained by the quantum optimizer on the *original unshrunk QUBO*.

Instance	Opt.	Qubits$_{QUBO}$	Qubits$_{Shrink}$	AGS	NGS	LGS	VQE
1dc.64	10	64	51	90.0	70.0	90.0	87.5
1et.64	18	64	46	88.9	55.6	100.0	77.8
1tc.16	8	16	9	87.5	50.0	87.5	75.0
1tc.32	12	32	20	100.0	66.7	91.7	75.0
1tc.64	20	64	43	90.0	70.0	100.0	40.0
1tc.8	4	8	4	100.0	100.0	100.0	100.0

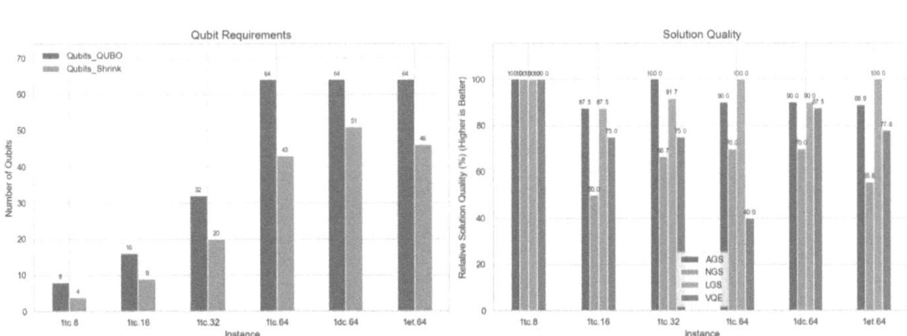

Fig. 2. Performance comparison on MIS benchmarks. The figure presents a side-by-side analysis of qubit requirements and solution quality for various methods across several Maximum Independent Set (MIS) instances. **(Left)** A comparison of the number of qubits required for the original QUBO formulation versus the reduced count after graph shrinking. **(Right)** The Relative Solution Quality (RSQ %), where higher values indicate better performance. The chart compares results from Adaptive (AGS), Naïve (NGS), and Learned (LGS) shrinking methods against the VQE solver on the original, unshrunk graph.

MDKP Results. For the Multi-Dimensional Knapsack Problem, where results are reported in **optimality gap (%)**, LGS consistently achieves the lowest or near-lowest gaps among all shrunk-graph baselines. In **pb2**, for example, LGS attains a gap of only 4.74%, outperforming AGS (11.49%) and NGS (48.40%), while using fewer than 60 qubits compared to over 100 required for the unshrunk VQE baseline. Even in complex, high-dimensional instances (e.g., **pet5**, **pet7**), LGS preserves feasible structures and produces high-quality solutions despite significant compression. These trends confirm that the learned policy generalizes effectively across problem sizes and constraint densities, learning correlations that approximate, and often surpass those obtained via SDP-based methods (Fig. 3).

7.2 Discussion

Unlike the handcrafted X_{SDP} matrix, the learned correlation estimator $X_{\mathrm{RL}}(i,j) = Q(s_t,(i,j);\theta)$ dynamically adapts to graph evolution and problem-specific constraints. Integrating X_{RL} into the graph shrinking pipeline yields real-time correlation estimation and substantial reductions in qubit usage, without sacrificing optimization quality. The combination of learning-based correlations, spectral stopping, and feasibility repair ensures that the shrunk problem instances remain representative of the original combinatorial structure, allowing downstream QAOA/VQE solvers to operate efficiently.

Table 2. Performance comparison on MDKP benchmarks. Reported values indicate the **Optimality Gap (%)**, computed as $\text{Gap} = 100 \times |f_{\text{final}} - f_{\text{opt}}| / f_{\text{opt}}$; lower values denote solutions closer to the optimum. **Qubits (QUBO)** corresponds to the number of qubits required for the original unshrunk QUBO, while **Qubits (Shrink)** denotes the reduced qubit count after graph shrinking. **AGS**, **NGS**, and **LGS** represent results obtained on *shrunk graphs* generated by Adaptive (SDP-based), Naïve (random), and Learned (RL-based, proposed) graph shrinking, respectively. **VQE** reports the optimality gap for the quantum solver on the *original unshrunk QUBO*. Missing entries (–) indicate solver failure or non-convergence.

Instance	Opt.	Qubits$_{\text{QUBO}}$	Qubits$_{\text{Shrink}}$	AGS	NGS	LGS	VQE
hp1	3418	60	50	15.77	40.37	9.54	39.76
hp2	3186	67	57	16.61	30.13	8.95	12.34
pb1	3090	59	50	12.92	45.57	2.88	19.94
pb2	3186	66	56	11.49	48.40	4.74	19.49
pb4	95168	45	37	11.41	25.53	18.34	–
pb5	2139	116	95	12.53	20.66	12.53	4.25
pet2	87061	99	80	0.21	85.56	2.90	41.07
pet3	4015	102	82	2.49	51.43	3.39	4.98
pet4	6120	107	85	16.99	51.14	2.16	66.58
pet5	12400	122	98	12.66	48.02	2.42	33.23
pet6	10618	86	72	7.23	22.30	10.10	12.50
pet7	16537	100	85	10.52	50.66	43.26	43.46

8   Outlook and Future Work

This work establishes reinforcement learning as an effective and scalable alternative to SDP-based correlation estimation in hybrid classicalquantum optimization. Several promising directions can further enhance adaptability, generalization, and quantum integration.

Meta-Reinforcement Learning and Policy Reuse. Future extensions will explore *Meta-RL* frameworks that enable the policy to self-improve across multiple problem classes through transfer and continual adaptation. Such meta-learned policies could reuse knowledge from previously solved instances, yielding faster convergence and improved performance on unseen graph structures.

Multi-Agent Learning for Distributed Shrinking. An alternative pathway involves *multi-agent coordination*, where several merge agents operate in parallel on distinct graph regions, exchanging local embeddings or correlation information. This decentralized formulation may better exploit structural locality, reduce decision latency, and scale efficiently to large problem instances.

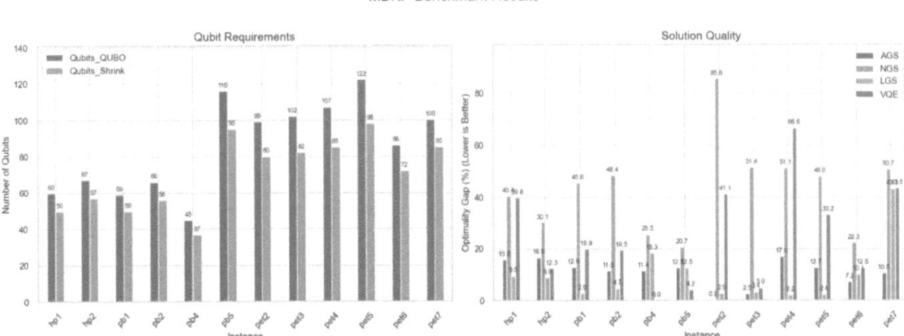

Fig. 3. Performance comparison on MDKP benchmarks. This figure illustrates the resource requirements and solution quality for several Multidimensional Knapsack Problem (MDKP) instances. **(Left)** The plot details the reduction in required qubits from the original QUBO to the shrunk problem formulation. **(Right)** A comparison of the Optimality Gap (%), where lower values signify solutions closer to the optimum. Performance is shown for the Adaptive (AGS), Naïve (NGS), and Learned (LGS) methods on shrunk graphs, as well as for the VQE solver on the original problem.

Integration with Online Quantum Pipelines. Finally, integrating the learned shrinking policy into *online quantum pipelines* opens new opportunities for adaptive, real-time preprocessing on quantum hardware. By coupling RL-based correlation estimation with QAOA/VQE solvers and feedback from hardware execution, the system could dynamically adjust merge strategies based on empirical noise profiles, circuit depth constraints, and qubit connectivity.

Comparative Evaluation with Classical Coarsening. Future work will benchmark the proposed method against classical coarsening approaches such as METIS [34] and Graclus [35] to contextualize its efficiency and scalability.

Overall, these directions point toward a self-improving, hardware-aware framework that unites learning-based preprocessing, distributed coordination, and adaptive quantum execution within a unified hybrid optimization paradigm.

References

1. Juan, A.A., Faulin, J., Grasman, S.E., Rabe, M., Figueira, G.: A review of simheuristics: extending metaheuristics to deal with stochastic combinatorial optimization problems. Oper. Res. Perspect. **2**, 62–72 (2015)
2. Du, D., Pardalos, P.M.: Handbook of Combinatorial Optimization. Springer, Cham (1998)
3. Bengio, Y., Lodi, A., Prouvost, A.: Machine learning for combinatorial optimization: a methodological tour d'horizon. Eur. J. Oper. Res. **290**(2), 405–421 (2021)
4. Kumar, M., Sharma, A., Kumar, S.: A unified framework for optimization-based graph coarsening. J. Mach. Learn. Res. **24**(118), 1–50 (2023)

5. Jin, Y., Loukas, A., Joseph, J.: Graph coarsening with preserved spectral properties (2020)
6. Loukas, A., Vandergheynst, P.: Spectrally approximating large graphs with smaller graphs (2018)
7. Dey, T.K., Peng, P., Rossi, A., Sidiropoulos, A.: Spectral concentration and greedy k-clustering (2018) https://arxiv.org/abs/1404.1008
8. Allen, C., Pashkov, N., Goldstein, O., Keller, G.: Learning Markov state abstractions for deep reinforcement learning. Adv. Neural. Inf. Process. Syst. **34**, 8229–8241 (2021)
9. Darvariu, V.-A., Hanneke, S., Mirco, M.: Graph reinforcement learning for combinatorial optimization: a survey and unifying perspective (2024)
10. Darvariu, V.-A., Hailes, S., Musolesi, M.: Goal-directed graph construction using reinforcement learning. Proc. R. Soc. A **477**(2254), 20210168 (2021)
11. SMU Quantum Computing Group: Quantum Optimization Benchmarks. (2025). https://github.com/SMU-Quantum/quantum-optimization-benchmarks
12. Chen, J., Saad, Y., Zhang, Z.: Graph coarsening: from scientific computing to machine learning. SeMA J. **79**(1), 187–223 (2022). https://doi.org/10.1007/s40324-021-00282-x
13. Zhou, J., Cui, G., Hu, S., Zhang, Z., Yang, C., Liu, Z., Wang, L., Li, C., Sun, M.: Graph neural networks: a review of methods and applications. AI Open **1**, 57–81 (2020)
14. Cappart, Q., Chételat, D., Khalil, E.B., Lodi, A., Morris, C., Veličković, P.: Combinatorial optimization and reasoning with graph neural networks. J. Mach. Learn. Res. **24**(130), 1–61 (2023)
15. Zhang, X.-M., Liang, L., Liu, L., Tang, M.-J.: Graph neural networks and their current applications in bioinformatics. Front. Genet. **12**, 690049 (2021)
16. Tönshoff, J., Kisin, B., Lindner, J., Grohe, M.: One model, any CSP: graph neural networks as fast global search heuristics for constraint satisfaction. arXiv preprint arXiv:2208.10227 (2022)
17. Fan, J., Wang, Z., Xie, Y., Yang, Z.: A theoretical analysis of deep Q-learning. In: Proceedings of the Learning for Dynamics and Control Conference, pp. 486–489. PMLR (2020)
18. Van Hasselt, H., Guez, A., Silver, D.: Deep reinforcement learning with double Q-learning. In: Proceedings of the AAAI Conference on Artificial Intelligence, vol. 30, no. 1 (2016)
19. Peng, Y., Choi, B., Xu, J.: Graph learning for combinatorial optimization: a survey of state-of-the-art. Data Sci. Eng. **6**(2), 119–141 (2021)
20. Farhi, E., Goldstone, J., Gutmann, S.: A quantum approximate optimization algorithm (2014). https://arxiv.org/abs/1411.4028
21. Peruzzo, A., et al.: A variational eigenvalue solver on a photonic quantum processor. Nat. Commun. **5**(1), 4213 (2014)
22. Fischer, V., Passek, M., Wagner, F., Finžgar, J.R., Palackal, L., Mendl: quantum and classical correlations in shrinking algorithms for optimization (2024). https://arxiv.org/abs/2404.17242
23. Herzog, L.S., et al.: Improving quantum and classical decomposition methods for vehicle routing (2024). https://arxiv.org/abs/2404.05551
24. Drake, J.H.: Benchmark instances for the Multidimensional Knapsack Problem. Available from ResearchGate (2015)
25. Sloane, N.J.A.: Challenge Problems: Independent Sets in Graphs (2000). https://oeis.org/A265032/a265032.html

26. Kellerer, H., Pferschy, U., Pisinger, D.: Multidimensional Knapsack Problems. Springer, Cham (2004)
27. Tarjan, R.E., Trojanowski, A.E.: Finding a maximum independent set. SIAM J. Comput. **6**(3), 537–546 (1977)
28. Sharma, M., Lau, H.C.: Adaptive graph shrinking for quantum optimization of constrained combinatorial problems. arXiv preprint arXiv:2506.14250 (2025)
29. Khot, S., Kindler, G., Mossel, E., O'Donnell, R.: Optimal inapproximability results for MAX-CUT and other 2-variable CSPs. SIAM J. Comput. **37**(1), 319–357 (2007)
30. Castelvecchi, D.: IBM releases first-ever 1,000-qubit quantum chip. Nature **624**(7991), 238 (2023)
31. IBM Newsroom: IBM Unveils 400+ Qubit Quantum Processor and Next-Generation IBM Quantum System Two (2022). https://tinyurl.com/watvte8x
32. RIKEN News: RIKEN and Fujitsu Begin Operation of 256-Qubit Superconducting Quantum Computer (2025). https://www.riken.jp/en/news_pubs/news/2025/20250422_1/index.html
33. Quantinuum Blog: Introducing Helios: The Most Accurate Quantum Computer in the World (2024). https://www.quantinuum.com/blog/introducing-helios-the-most-accurate-quantum-computer-in-the-world
34. Karypis, G., Kumar, V.: A fast and high quality multilevel scheme for partitioning irregular graphs. SIAM J. Sci. Comput. **20**(1), 359–392 (1998)
35. Dhillon, I.S., Guan, Y., Kulis, B.: Weighted graph cuts without eigenvectors: a multilevel approach. IEEE Trans. Pattern Anal. Mach. Intell. **29**(11), 1944–1957 (2007)

Hybrid Quantum–Classical Framework
for Acute Hypotension Control

Hrvoje Kukina[(✉)] and Clemens Heitzinger

TU Wien, Vienna, Austria
`hrvoje.kukina@student.tuwien.ac.at`, `clemens.heitzinger@tuwien.ac.at`

Abstract. We present a hybrid quantum–classical Deep Q-Learning framework for short-horizon blood-pressure control and evaluate it in a reproducible environment derived from openly released, de-identified ICU trajectories. Our approach inserts a variational quantum circuit as a nonlinear feature map inside an otherwise standard DQN pipeline, keeping replay, target networks, and ϵ-greedy exploration unchanged to enable fair comparisons with classical baselines. Taken together, the results provide an open, lightweight testbed and a competitive baseline for studying quantum-enhanced function approximation in safety-critical sequential decision making, while clarifying where hybrid models can add value without claiming absolute quantum advantage.

Keywords: hypotension control · variational quantum circuit · deep Q-learning

1 Introduction

Data-driven decision support systems are increasingly used to assist high-frequency clinical control tasks. When observations and interventions arrive as a stream and actions influence future measurements, reinforcement learning (RL) [24] provides a natural framework to learn policies that optimize long-run outcomes. However, demonstrating practical value in healthcare requires reproducible environments [7], transparent baselines, and careful comparisons that separate modeling choices from data and reward design.

To enable such comparisons for blood-pressure targeting, we build on the publicly released Health Gym [18] hypotension environment, which offers a standardized state–action–reward interface derived from de-identified ICU trajectories [12]. While recent work has explored both a range of classical value-based agents in this setting [15,19,20] and the intersection between parameterized quantum circuits and reinforcement learning [4,14,23], there is limited controlled evidence that hybrid quantum–classical models can serve as effective function approximators for RL in clinical control problems under matched training protocols [8].

This paper investigates a compact hybrid Deep Q-Network (QC-DQN) that inserts a variational quantum circuit as a nonlinear feature map within an otherwise classical DQN scaffold. The goal is not to claim quantum advantage in

S. Ali et al. (Eds.): QC+AI 2026, CCIS 2872, pp. 50–65, 2026.
https://doi.org/10.1007/978-3-032-17625-7_4

an absolute sense, but to assess whether such hybrids can deliver competitive stability and sample efficiency on a clinically motivated control task, given the same replay, target-network, and exploration schedules used by strong classical baselines.

Contributions. Our work offers:

- A lightweight, open RL setup for short-horizon blood-pressure control compatible with Health-Gym-style trajectories, with clearly specified preprocessing, action grids, and reward shaping for reproducible evaluation.
- A principled QC-DQN architecture that employs angle embedding, entangling layers, and Pauli-Z readouts as a bounded feature map feeding a linear action head, trained end-to-end with experience replay and a fixed target network.
- A controlled empirical study that matches capacity and training hyperparameters across QC-DQN and classical DQN, reporting return, time in target band, and extremes-avoidance metrics, alongside ablations on circuit depth and embedding choices.

By emphasizing a clear, reproducible pipeline, we aim to establish a practical baseline for assessing hybrid quantum–classical RL in safety-critical control.

Section 2 covers the clinical background. Sections 4–7 detail the environment and the QC–DQN design. Sections 8–9 present results and ablations, followed by conclusion and future directions in Section X.

2   Acute Hypotension

Acute hypotension is commonly understood as an abrupt and clinically significant fall in arterial pressure that threatens tissue perfusion and risks ischemic injury to vital organs [3]. In the ICU, it arises from heterogeneous etiologies (e.g., sepsis, hemorrhage, cardiogenic shock, anesthetic effects), and bedside management prioritizes rapid stabilization of mean arterial pressure with crystalloid resuscitation and titrated vasopressors while clinicians track frequent vital signs, laboratory panels, and urine output.[1] Because interventions are delivered and adjusted over time, as new measurements arrive and patient response unfolds, the clinical scenario is naturally cast as a sequential decision problem rather than a single-shot choice, motivating reinforcement learning (RL) and related temporal models for methods research [18].

To enable open, reproducible benchmarking without exposing protected health information, the Health Gym project released a synthetic acute hypotension dataset generated from a cohort in MIMIC-III using generative adversarial networks (GANs) [18]. The GAN is trained to capture the joint distribution of discretized trajectories (vital signs, labs, and interventions such as fluids and vasopressors) together with clinically meaningful outcomes, producing cohorts that mirror the statistical structure of the source population while containing

---

[1] In many protocols a MAP target of $\approx 65\,\mathrm{mmHg}$ is used as an initial goal, with subsequent individualization; see guideline discussions summarized in [6].

no direct patient identifiers. The released environment provides state vectors with physiologic and treatment features, action spaces reflecting typical clinical choices (fluid/vasopressor bins), and reward definitions tied to MAP control and safety terms—elements specifically tailored for evaluating offline RL and policy-learning algorithms on ICU-like dynamics [18].

Importantly, the creators report low disclosure risk following their privacy assessment: empirical similarity and membership-inference analyses did not indicate memorization of individuals, and summary statistics and model-based audits suggested that the synthetic samples generalize attributes of the original cohort rather than reproducing records verbatim [12,18]. In practice, this strikes a balance between methodological realism (trajectory-level dependence, action–outcome couplings) and open accessibility, allowing researchers to compare algorithms under shared preprocessing and reward conventions, probe robustness to distribution shift and counterfactual evaluation, and share code and reproducible results without restricted data-use agreements—all while safeguarding patient privacy [12].

3   Dataset

3.1   Cohort and Scope

This paper uses a longitudinal, patient-time series hypotension dataset comprising 3,910 unique ICU patients observed uniformly over 48 discrete timepoints, yielding 187,680 patient-hours of observation. This dataset provides a large, balanced, and physiologically coherent panel suitable for developing and validating predictive models of hypotension and related adverse states in the early phase of critical illness. Timepoints are indexed from 0 to 47 and represent equally spaced sampling intervals; for clinical interpretability we treat them as hourly measures over the first 48 h of index care. Each row corresponds to a single patient-time record and is uniquely identified by the composite key (PatientID, Timepoints). Variables include mean arterial, systolic, and diastolic blood pressures; key laboratory values (e.g., lactate, creatinine, liver enzymes); ventilatory parameters (PaO_2, FiO_2); urine output; neurological status (GCS); and administered fluid boluses and vasopressors. The dataset also carries binary indicators that mark whether a measurement occurred at a given hour—useful signals in clinical time-series. [18] Because fluids and vasopressors appear alongside rich state variables, the dataset naturally supports an RL formulation where actions are (discretized) treatment choices and states are the evolving physiologic profile; this design follows the cohort definition introduced by Gottesman et al. and adapted by Health Gym. The open, synthetic release addresses long-standing barriers to sharing ICU data, creating a standard testbed for comparing algorithms under identical conditions.

This dataset structure enables both cross-sectional and temporal modeling of hypotension risk. The balanced window of 48 h captures the early clinical trajectory when hemodynamic instability, interventions (fluids, vasopressors), and evolving organ dysfunction are most dynamic. Incorporating m flags preserves information about data generation and imputation—signals that have been shown to improve predictive performance in clinical time-series models.

3.2 Variables

The dataset contains 23 columns spanning hemodynamics, respiratory support, neurologic status, laboratory markers, therapies, and missingness indicators:

- Hemodynamics: Mean arterial pressure (MAP), systolic blood pressure (SBP), and diastolic blood pressure (DBP), recorded as continuous variables.
- Renal and fluids: Hourly urine output (urine) and discrete volumes of fluid boluses administered at that timepoint (fluid boluses, commonly 0, 250, 500, or 1000 mL) [16].
- Liver enzymes: Alanine aminotransferase (ALT) and aspartate aminotransferase (AST).
- Oxygenation and ventilatory support: Partial pressure of arterial oxygen (PaO_2) and fraction of inspired oxygen (FiO_2, reported on 0–1 scale).
- Neurologic status: Glasgow Coma Scale total score (GCS total, range 3–15).
- Metabolic and kidney function: Lactic acid and serum creatinine.
- Vasoactive therapy: vasopressors, a continuous proxy for dose/intensity (zero-inflated, reflecting on-/off-support).
- Missingness flags: Binary indicators for urine, ALT/AST, FiO_2, GCS, PO_2, lactic acid, and creatinine. Although the analytic table contains no NaNs, these flags denote whether the corresponding measurement was originally missing and subsequently imputed (1) versus observed (0), a common convention in clinical datasets and a useful signal for downstream models.

3.3 Outcome Definition

The primary physiologic endpoint is hypotension defined by the conventional threshold MAP < 65 mmHg [1]. A binary label was derived at each timepoint as

$$Hypotensive_{i,t} = 1\{MAP_{i,t} < 65\}. \tag{1}$$

Across all patient-time observations, approximately 48.4% meet this criterion, with a higher prevalence early in the time series.

3.4 Descriptive Characteristics

Hemodynamic variables exhibit clinically plausible central tendencies: MAP averages 65.2 ± 9.3 mmHg (range $\sim$ 19.4–122.6), with corresponding SBP 112.6 $\pm$ 14.0 mmHg and DBP 54.5 $\pm$ 9.4 mmHg. FiO_2 has a median of 0.5, and PO_2 averages $\sim 104 \pm 21.5$ mmHg. Neurologic status is generally preserved (median GCS total = 15, IQR 11–15). Metabolic and renal markers cluster around lactic acid $\sim 1.60 \pm 0.46$ mmol/L and serum creatinine $\sim 1.30 \pm 0.69$ mg/dL. Interventions are intermittently applied: vasopressors > 0 occur in $\sim 15.9\%$ of timepoints, while fluid boluses > 0 are less frequent ($\sim 2.7\%$), typically in discrete 250–1000 mL increments. Pairwise associations align with physiologic expectations. MAP correlates strongly with DBP ($r \approx 0.80$) and, to a lesser degree, SBP ($r \approx 0.59$). We observe weaker negative associations between MAP and FiO_2 (~ -0.09), fluid boluses (~ -0.06), and serum creatinine (~ -0.15), consistent with lower perfusion pressures co-occurring with higher oxygen requirements, fluid resuscitation, and renal dysfunction.

3.5   Preprocessing

Data preparation in our implementation closely follows what the environment code actually performs. After loading the Health-Gym CSV, we first remove any non-informative index columns whose names begin with `Unnamed` and sort the table by `PatientID` and `Timepoints` to restore episode order. Because the raw vasopressor field in Health-Gym often contains tiny numerical noise around zero, values with magnitude at most 10^{-3} are collapsed to 0, producing a cleaner baseline "no pressor" level. Discrete action bins for fluids and vasopressors are then inferred directly from the data as the unique sorted values of `fluid_boluses` and `vasopressors`, and for each row we compute the nearest-bin indices `FluidLoggedBin` and `VasoLoggedBin`. The observation vector is formed from the subset of physiologic variables present in the CSV (including, when available, `MAP`, `diastolic_bp`, `systolic_bp`, `urine`, `lactic_acid`, `serum_creatinine`, `FiO2`, `GCS_total`, `ALT`, `AST`, `PO2`), and we optionally include missingness indicators by selecting any columns that end with `_m`. We also append the derived previous-action features `FluidPrevBin` and `VasoPrevBin`; if any feature in the observation set is absent in the CSV, the column is created and initialized to zero to maintain a consistent schema. Feature scaling parameters (means μ and standard deviations σ) are estimated over the observation columns, and each observation is standardized at runtime via $z = (x - \mu)/\sigma$ with per-feature clipping to $[-8, 8]$ to bound outliers.

3.6   Limitations

Two caveats merit note. First, therapy variables (vasopressors, fluid boluses) reflect concurrent management and may introduce treatment-confounding if used naively for causal inference; modeling should account for time-varying confounding (e.g., marginal structural models) when appropriate. Second, while units follow common clinical conventions, they are inferred from context rather than explicitly encoded in the file; downstream analyses should document unit assumptions and perform sensitivity checks.

4   Acute Hypotension Control Environment

We developed a reinforcement learning environment for acute hypotension management that is aligned with the Health-Gym tabular schema and operates directly on CSV trajectories. The environment models the short-horizon control of mean arterial pressure using two interventions: intravenous fluids and vasopressors. It is implemented with the (legacy) OpenAI Gym API [2], enabling straightforward integration with common RL baselines.

4.1 Data Interface and Prerequisites

The environment consumes a single CSV with required columns: PatientID, Timepoints, MAP, fluid boluses, vasopressors and optional observational covariates (diastolic bp, systolic bp, urine, lactic acid, serum creatinine, FiO_2, GCS total, ALT, AST, PO_2) as well as any binary missingness indicators. Upon load, any spurious index columns (e.g., Unnamed:*) are dropped, trajectories are sorted by (PatientID, Timepoints), and tiny vasopressor magnitudes ($|dose|$ $\leq$ `1e-3`) are collapsed to 0 to harmonize dose coding commonly seen in Health-Gym datasets.

4.2 Action Space

Actions are discrete and represent a Cartesian product of binned fluids and vasopressor levels. Rather than imposing fixed bins, we infer bins from the data:

- fluids levels := sorted unique values of fluid boluses in the CSV (or user-supplied),
- vaso levels := sorted unique values of vasopressors in the CSV (or user-supplied, with near-zeros collapsed to 0)

If the inferred cardinalities are f_{bins} and v_{bins} (each ≥ 2), the action space has size $f_{bins} \times v_{bins}$. This asymmetric discretization respects the empirical dose grid, preserves clinically used increments (e.g., 0, 250, 500, 1000 mL), and avoids empty or implausible action cells.

4.3 State (Observation) Representation

At each time t, the observable state consists of all available clinical covariates present in the CSV from the set: MAP, DBP, SBP, urine, lactate, creatinine, FiO_2, GCS, ALT, AST, PO_2, plus any m missingness flags (if enabled), and two derived features encoding the immediately previous action in bin space: `FluidPrevBin` and `VasoPrevBin`. Absent columns are created and filled with zeros to maintain a consistent observation vector across datasets. Observations are standardized as

$$z = \text{clip}\left(\frac{x - \mu}{\sigma}, -8, 8\right),$$

where μ and σ are the empirical mean and standard deviation computed over the training table for the chosen feature set. Clipping curtails the influence of extreme values while preserving rank information.

4.4 Logged Policies and Bin Alignment

For counterfactual reasoning, the environment computes the logged action bins taken in the data at time t: `FluidLoggedBin` and `VasoLoggedBin`, defined as nearest-neighbor indices to the dataset's level grids. These serve as a reference against which new policy choices are contrasted.

The next state is anchored to the observed trajectory and then adjusted in MAP by a linear response to deviations from the logged bins. Let $a_t = (f_t, v_t)$ be the chosen bins and $(\tilde{f}_t, \tilde{v}_t)$ the logged bins. Let $\mathrm{MAP}^{\mathrm{logged}}_{t+1}$ be the next-step MAP in the dataset. The counterfactual MAP used for the transition is

$$\mathrm{MAP}^{\mathrm{cf}}_{t+1} = \mathrm{MAP}^{\mathrm{logged}}_{t+1} + \alpha_{\mathrm{fluid}}\left(f_t - \tilde{f}_t\right) + \alpha_{\mathrm{vaso}}\left(v_t - \tilde{v}_t\right),$$

with default sensitivities $\alpha_{\mathrm{fluid}} = 1.5$ and $\alpha_{\mathrm{vaso}} = 3.0$. All other covariates of the next state follow the logged values (i.e., a semi-parametric, one-step adjustment limited to MAP). The derived features `FluidPrevBin`/`VasoPrevBin` are updated to the action just taken. This design preserves the high-dimensional temporal structure of real trajectories while introducing a transparent, tunable counterfactual mechanism on the target physiology.

4.5 Reward Shaping and Safety Penalties

Rewards target a clinically desirable MAP band and discourage unsafe excursions and overly aggressive treatment:

- Primary target band: MAP $\in$ [target low, target high] $= [65,75]$ yields $+1$.
- Smooth shaping outside target:

$$r_{\mathrm{shape}} = 1 - \min\{2.5,\ |MAP - 70|/10\},$$

  which declines linearly from the nominal setpoint 70 and floors at -1.5.
- Safety terms: additional -1.0 if MAP $<$ unsafe low $= 50$; and -0.3 if MAP $>$ higher high $= 90$.
- Treatment regularization: small action costs scaled to bin indices,

$$r_{\mathrm{tx}} = -0.01\,\frac{f_t}{\max(1, f_{\mathrm{bins}} - 1)} - 0.05\,\frac{v_t}{\max(1, v_{\mathrm{bins}} - 1)},$$

  reflecting a higher propensity for adverse effects or resource use with increasing vasopressor intensity and fluid volume.

The total reward is the sum of the applicable components evaluated on $\mathrm{MAP}^{\mathrm{cf}}_{t+1}$.

4.6   Episodes

Episodes correspond to patient trajectories. On reset(), a patient is sampled uniformly at random (seed-controlled), the index is set to the first row, and previous-action features are initialized to the logged first-step bins (falling back to zero if absent). At each step, the environment advances by one row. Termination occurs at the final timepoint for that patient or when a configurable cap is reached (max episode steps=48 by default), matching typical 48-hour windows in ICU datasets.

The environment strikes a balance between realism and controllability. The data-driven action grid respects clinical practice patterns and avoids unpopulated bins that complicate off-policy evaluation. The linear counterfactual isolates the primary physiological target for which mechanistic monotonicity with interventions is broadly accepted: vasopressors predominantly raise MAP; fluids can raise MAP with smaller marginal effect sizes. The reward encodes bedside goals (maintain MAP $\geq$ 65 mmHg) while discouraging both hypotension and excessive hypertension, and modestly regularizes treatment intensity to reflect risk/benefit trade-offs.

5   Deep Q-Learning

Deep Q-Networks (DQN) extend classical Q-learning by combining value-based reinforcement learning with deep function approximation and several stabilization techniques. A deep neural network is trained to approximate the action-value function $Q(s, a)$. Instead of updating from only the most recent transition, the algorithm draws mini-batches of transitions sampled from a replay buffer, which helps to reduce temporal correlations in the training data. In addition, DQN maintains a separate target network whose parameters are updated only periodically and are used to compute the next-state targets, improving the stability of learning [17].

Numerous variants build on this framework, such as Double DQN and dueling architectures, but they all rely on a neural network that maps a (possibly high-dimensional) state representation to a vector of Q-values, one for each available action [9,25]. Q-learning, a conventional reinforcement-learning algorithm, centers on estimating a Q-value. A Q-value indicates the expected cumulative reward an agent can obtain by taking a specific action in a given state under a particular policy. The primary goal is to learn an optimal Q-function that guides the agent to make choices that maximize total cumulative reward. In a typical DQN implementation, the agent maintains a replay buffer containing its most recent interactions with the environment. Each stored transition can be represented as a five-tuple $(s_t, a_t, r_t, s_{t+1}, done)$, encoding the current state, the action taken, the immediate reward, the next state, and a terminal flag. After every environment step, the new transition is appended to this memory, and learning updates are performed on mini-batches of transitions sampled from the buffer. This experience replay mechanism allows the agent to reuse past interactions for multiple updates, breaks the strong temporal correlations present in sequential data, and has been shown to improve both the data efficiency and stability of learning in DQN [17]. In experience replay, the key idea is that the agent does not train only on the latest transition, but instead saves and selectively retrieves past experiences from this replay buffer. By sampling transitions at random, rather than in the order they were observed, the algorithm weakens the sequential correlation between samples and presents the neural network with a more diverse and representative set of training instances. This leads to more robust learning and better generalization. DQN also employs a separate set of (older) network parameters to compute the target Q-values for the next state, and these parameters are updated only at regular intervals spanning many steps. This target network approach gives the main network time to adjust to its current targets and helps to reduce instability and oscillations in the value estimates during training [17]. The DQN loss function is based on the temporal-difference (TD) error, which measures the discrepancy between the current Q-value estimate and a target estimate constructed from the observed reward and the target network's prediction for the next state. The neural network is trained to minimize this TD loss by adjusting its parameters so that its predicted Q-values more closely match the targets, thereby moving the learned Q-function toward the optimal one. Finally, DQN typically uses an epsilon-greedy strategy to balance exploration and exploitation. With probability ϵ, the agent selects a random action to explore the environment; with probability $1 - \epsilon$, it selects the action that currently has the highest predicted Q-value. This mixture promotes the discovery of potentially better actions while still leveraging the knowledge encoded in the learned Q-function.

6   Classical Hypotension Control

We employ a classical feed-forward DQN with two hidden layers:

$$Q_\theta(s, a) := [\phi_\theta(s)]_a \,, \quad \phi_\theta(s) = \mathrm{MLP}_{256 \to 256 \to |\mathcal{A}|}(s),$$

with ReLU activations between linear layers. Two networks are maintained: an *online* network Q_θ (updated every gradient step) and a *target* network $Q_{\bar{\theta}}$ (held fixed between periodic synchronizations). The target parameters are hard-synced to the online parameters every C environment steps (`target_sync=100`):

$$\bar{\theta} \leftarrow \theta \quad \text{every } C \text{ steps.}$$

Experience Replay. We use a first-in–first-out replay buffer $\mathcal{D}$ of capacity $N =$ `replay_size=10,000` that stores transitions

$$(s_t, a_t, r_t, s_{t+1}, d_t) \in \mathcal{S} \times \mathcal{A} \times \mathbb{R} \times \mathcal{S} \times \{0, 1\},$$

where $d_t = 1$ indicates episode termination. Learning commences only after a warm-up of `min_replay=1000` collected transitions to ensure sufficiently diverse mini-batches [13].

Action Selection: ε-Greedy Exploration. Actions are selected with an ε-greedy policy w.r.t. the online network:

$$\pi_\varepsilon(a \mid s) = \begin{cases} \mathrm{Unif}(\mathcal{A}) & \text{with prob. } \varepsilon, \\ \arg\max_{a'} Q_\theta(s, a') & \text{with prob. } 1 - \varepsilon. \end{cases}$$

We anneal ε linearly across episodes from $\varepsilon_{\text{start}}{=}1.0$ to $\varepsilon_{\text{final}}{=}0.01$ over $E_{\text{decay}}{=}800$ episodes:

$$\varepsilon(e) = \varepsilon_{\text{final}} + \left(\varepsilon_{\text{start}} - \varepsilon_{\text{final}}\right) \cdot \max\left(0, \frac{E_{\text{decay}} - e}{E_{\text{decay}}}\right).$$

Learning Objective and Optimization. Given a sampled mini-batch $\{(s_i, a_i, r_i, s'_i, d_i)\}_{i=1}^{B}$ from $\mathcal{D}$ with $B = \texttt{batch\_size}{=}64$, we form the standard DQN target using the *target* network to evaluate next-state values:

$$y_i = r_i + \gamma\,(1 - d_i)\,\max_{a'} Q_{\bar{\theta}}(s'_i, a'), \qquad \gamma = 0.99.$$

The online network is trained to minimize the mean-squared Bellman error

$$\mathcal{L}(\theta) = \frac{1}{B}\sum_{i=1}^{B}\left(Q_\theta(s_i, a_i) - y_i\right)^2.$$

We optimize θ using Adam [11] with learning rate $\eta = \texttt{lr} = 10^{-3}$.

Training Loop and Runtime Details. Training proceeds for $\texttt{max\_episodes}{=}1000$ episodes. Within each episode, we iterate environment steps until termination (or $\texttt{max\_episode\_steps}$). At each step: select an ε-greedy action; observe (r, s', d); push the transition to $\mathcal{D}$; if $|\mathcal{D}| > \texttt{min\_replay}$, sample a mini-batch and update θ via one gradient step; and every C steps, synchronize $\bar{\theta} \leftarrow \theta$. We record the undiscounted per-episode return to monitor learning stability.

The combination of a fixed target network and experience replay addresses two core instabilities in Q-learning: moving targets and correlated samples. The target network slows the drift of the bootstrap target y_i, while replay decorrelates updates by mixing transitions from disparate episodes and timepoints. The ε schedule front-loads exploration to populate the replay buffer before exploiting learned value structure.

7 Hybrid Quantum–Classical Hypotension Control

The proposed hybrid Q-network integrates a compact variational quantum circuit into a standard DQN pipeline. States are compressed to n_q features, encoded via R_Y rotations, processed by entangling layers, and read out through Pauli-Z expectations. A linear head maps quantum features to action values. Training proceeds with experience replay, a fixed target network, and ε-greedy exploration, optimizing the mean-squared Bellman error end-to-end. This yields a reproducible, hardware-aware quantum RL baseline for MAP control that is directly comparable to its classical counterpart.

Quantum Circuit. We use $n_{\mathrm{qubits}}{=}4$ qubits and $n_{\mathrm{layers}}{=}4$ layers on a `default.qubit` simulator. The QNode takes an input vector $x \in \mathbb{R}^{n_{\mathrm{qubits}}}$ (produced by a pre-network) and a trainable weight tensor $W \in \mathbb{R}^{L \times Q \times 3}$ with $L = n_{\mathrm{layers}}$ and $Q = n_{\mathrm{qubits}}$.

State Preparation (Encoding). Inputs are embedded with Y-rotations (AngleEmbedding):

$$|\psi_0\rangle \;=\; \bigotimes_{i=1}^{Q} R_Y(x_i)|0\rangle \quad \in (\mathbb{C}^2)^{\otimes Q}.$$

Parameterized Entangling Blocks. We apply L "Strongly Entangling" layers. Each layer ℓ consists of local Euler rotations on every qubit (three parameters per qubit) followed by a fixed entangling pattern (e.g. a ring of CNOTs):

$$|\psi_\ell\rangle \;=\; U_{\mathrm{ent}}\left(\bigotimes_{i=1}^{Q} R(W_{\ell,i,1}, W_{\ell,i,2}, W_{\ell,i,3})\right)|\psi_{\ell-1}\rangle,$$

$$\ell = 1, \ldots, L,$$

where $R(\cdot)$ denotes a sequence of single-qubit rotations and U_{ent} the entangler. The total number of circuit parameters is $3QL$.

Measurements. The circuit outputs expectation values of Pauli-Z on each qubit:

$$z \;=\; \big(\langle Z_1\rangle, \ldots, \langle Z_Q\rangle\big) \;\in\; [-1,1]^Q, \quad \langle Z_i\rangle \;=\; \langle\psi_L|Z_i|\psi_L\rangle.$$

We measure local Pauli-Z expectations,

$$z_i(x;\Theta) = \langle 0| U(\Theta,x)^\dagger Z_i\, U(\Theta,x)|0\rangle \in [-1,1], \quad i = 1, \ldots, n_q,$$

to obtain a quantum feature vector $z(x;\Theta) \in \mathbb{R}^{n_q}$. The trainable tensor has shape $\Theta \in \mathbb{R}^{L \times n_q \times 3}$ (three rotation parameters per qubit per layer), matching `weight_shapes={weights:(L, n_q, 3)}`.

Hybrid Q-Network Architecture. Let the environment state be $s \in \mathbb{R}^{d_{\mathrm{state}}}$ and the number of actions be n_{actions}.

1. Pre-net (classical):

$$x = \mathrm{ReLU}\big(W_{\mathrm{pre}}s + b_{\mathrm{pre}}\big) \in \mathbb{R}^Q.$$

This matches the circuit's required input dimension.

2. Quantum layer (QNode):

$$q = \mathrm{QNode}(x;\,W) = z \in \mathbb{R}^Q.$$

3. Head (classical):

$$Q(s, \cdot) = W_{\text{head}}q + b_{\text{head}} \in \mathbb{R}^{n_{\text{actions}}},$$

producing action-values (Q-values).

$$\underbrace{s \xrightarrow{\text{Linear+ReLU}} x \in \mathbb{R}^{n_q}}_{\text{pre-net}} \implies \underbrace{z(x;\Theta) \in \mathbb{R}^{n_q}}_{\text{quantum layer}}$$

$$\implies \underbrace{Q_\theta(s) = Wz + b \in \mathbb{R}^{|\mathcal{A}|}}_{\text{linear head}}.$$

Concretely, the pre-net is a single affine layer $\mathbb{R}^{d_s} \to \mathbb{R}^{n_q}$ with ReLU, providing dimension reduction and feature smoothing; the quantum layer is a PennyLane `TorchLayer` wrapping the QNode described above; and the head is a linear map $\mathbb{R}^{n_q} \to \mathbb{R}^{|\mathcal{A}|}$. We instantiate *online* and *target* copies of this hybrid network and hard-sync their parameters every C environment steps, as in classical DQN:

$$\bar{\theta} \leftarrow \theta \quad \text{when } t \bmod C = 0.$$

Experience Replay and Exploration. We maintain a FIFO replay buffer $\mathcal{D}$ of capacity N_{replay} that stores tuples $(s_t, a_t, r_t, s_{t+1}, d_t)$, where $d_t \in \{0, 1\}$ flags terminal transitions. Learning is deferred until $|\mathcal{D}| > N_{\text{warmup}}$ to ensure diverse batches. Action selection follows an ε-greedy policy, the same as in the classical version.

Training Setup. Two instances of the network are maintained: the *online* network (optimized) and a periodically updated *target* network initialized by copying the online parameters: $\theta_{\text{target}} \leftarrow \theta_{\text{online}}$. The online network is trained with Adam (learning rate lr) and a replayed reward history, as in standard DQN-style training.

Learning Objective and Optimization. All parameters, classical (pre/head) and quantum (Θ), are trained end-to-end with Adam at learning rate η, leveraging the parameter-shift rule internally for unbiased gradients [22, 26] through quantum expectations. We track the undiscounted episode return for monitoring.

This architecture follows the "small quantum core" principle: a low-depth, few-qubit circuit acts as a nonlinear feature map, while classical layers handle dimension matching and action decoding. Angle embedding via R_Y rotations is data-efficient and hardware-friendly; the *StronglyEntanglingLayers* template supplies expressive, trainable entanglement patterns without manual gate design. The quantum outputs are bounded, well-conditioned features for the linear head, mitigating exploding values in the Q-function. Retaining the classical DQN scaffold (replay, target network, ε-greedy) ensures stability and comparability with established baselines, isolating any contribution of quantum feature processing.

With $n_q{=}4$ and $L{=}4$, the quantum layer introduces $L \times n_q \times 3(\text{angles}){=}48$ variational parameters and constant-time expectation evaluation per wire on a statevector simulator. The total hybrid parameter count remains modest, which helps reduce overfitting in data-limited regimes. Because only n_q features are emitted, the linear head is lightweight: $\mathcal{O}(n_q|\mathcal{A}|)$ weights. The pre-net ensures compatibility with arbitrary d_s without discarding information entirely.

8   Results

We evaluate greedy policies ($\epsilon{=}0$) learned in the Acute Hypotension environment over a fixed horizon of 47 steps. Primary outcomes include the per-episode return, fraction of steps with mean arterial pressure in the target band [65,75] (**pct_in_band**), severe hypotension <50 (**pct_<50**), hypertension >90 (**pct_>90**), and mean absolute deviation from the nominal setpoint 70 (**mean_abs_dev**). To characterize treatment style, we report average action usage in both bin space and native dose space for fluids and vasopressors. For context, we include a uniform random policy and a no-treatment (always-zero) policy.

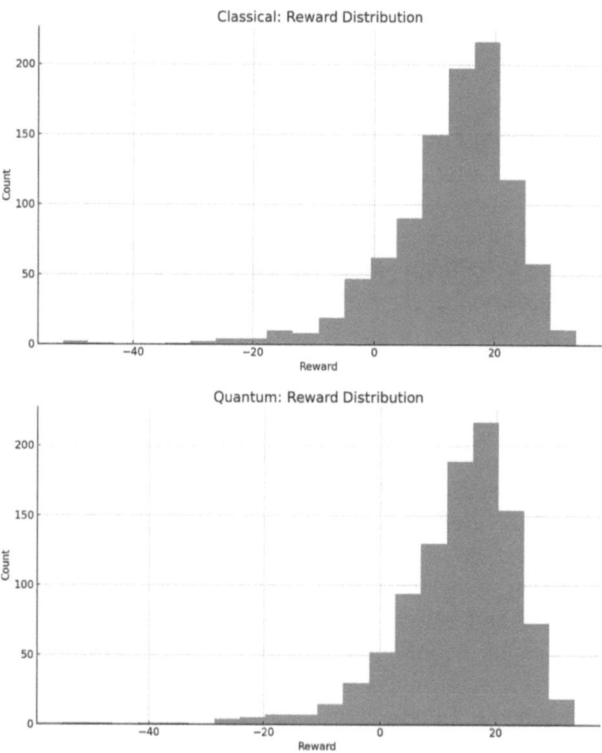

Fig. 1. Distribution of Episode Rewards for Classical and Quantum Agents.

Table 1. Performance summary of policies

Model	Steps[a]	Ret.[b]	In-band[c]	< 50[d]	> 90[e]	MAD[f]	Fluid bin[g]	Vaso bin[h]	Fluid lvl[i]	Vaso lvl[j]
Hybrid QC-DQN (greedy)	47.00	16.37	0.4366	0.0234	0.0136	7.25	2.97	0.013	988.83	0.118
Classical DQN (greedy)	47.00	13.42	0.4111	0.0247	0.0213	7.58	1.29	1.01	377.45	9.44
Baseline—Random	—	12.78	0.4004	0.0183	0.0243	7.80	—	—	437.98	9.45
Baseline—No-treatment	—	8.36	0.3719	0.0626	0.0081	8.55	—	—	—	—

[a] steps [b] return [c] pct_in_band [d] pct_<50 [e] pct_>90
[f] mean_abs_dev [g] mean_fluid_bin [h] mean_vaso_bin [i] mean_fluid_level [j] mean_vaso_level

Figure 1 shows the distribution of episode rewards obtained by the classical and quantum agents over 1,000 episodes each. Rewards are grouped into equally sized bins along the x-axis, and the height of each bar indicates how many episodes achieved a reward within that range. The quantum agent's distribution is slightly shifted toward higher rewards compared with the classical agent, reflecting its higher average return (Table 1).

The hybrid quantum agent attains a higher return and tighter MAP control than the classical DQN under identical evaluation:

- Return: $+2.95$ absolute (16.37 vs. 13.42).
- Time in band: $+2.55\%$ points (pp) (0.4366 vs. 0.4111).
- Severe hypotension <50: -0.13 pp (0.0234 vs. 0.0247).
- Hypertension >90: -0.77 pp (0.0136 vs. 0.0213).
- Tracking error: lower mean absolute deviation (7.25 vs. 7.58).

These differences indicate fewer unsafe excursions on both tails and a closer adherence to the clinical target band by the quantum-enhanced policy.

A salient distinction emerges in intervention mix [21]. The quantum policy is *fluid-forward* and *vasopressor-sparing* [5,10]:

fluids: 988.8 mL/step (QC) vs. 377.4 mL/step (classical)

vasopressors: 0.12 vs. 9.44

Given the reward includes small action regularizers with a higher penalty per vasopressor bin than per fluid bin, the quantum agent appears to discover a conservative strategy that elevates MAP predominantly via fluids, yielding fewer > 90 overshoots while maintaining low < 50 rates. By contrast, the classical DQN leans more on vasopressors and displays a higher incidence of hypertensive excursions.

Both learned policies outperform no-treatment by wide margins in return and safety (roughly halving severe hypotension from $\approx 6.3\%$ to ≈ 2.3–2.5%). Relative to random, the quantum agent delivers a clear improvement ($+3.59$ return; $+3.62$ pp in-band; -1.07 pp >90), whereas the classical agent is only marginally above random in return and in-band time, and exhibits similar vasopressor usage to random.

9 Conclusion

We introduced a hybrid quantum–classical Deep Q-Learning agent for short-horizon blood-pressure control and evaluated it in an open, reproducible environment aligned with Health-Gym conventions. Under matched training protocols, the hybrid QC-DQN achieved modest but consistent gains over a capacity-matched classical DQN. Higher returns, more time in the target MAP band, fewer hypertensive overshoots, and a fluid-forward, vasopressor-sparing policy suggest that a variational quantum circuit can serve as a useful nonlinear feature map within a stable DQN scaffold.

These findings indicate that quantum-enhanced representations can improve value estimation without altering standard RL infrastructure (replay, target networks, ϵ-greedy), thereby lowering the barrier to experimentation in safety-critical control tasks. The resulting pipeline is both promising and clinically plausible, providing a compact baseline for future comparisons and ablations. Future work will investigate scaling our architecture to larger VQCs and evaluating performance under hardware-level constraints to better understand practical quantum advantage. In parallel, we plan to introduce additional capacity-matched classical nonlinear baselines in place of the quantum layer to more clearly isolate the quantum layer's impact on policy performance.

References

1. Asfar, P., et al.: High versus low blood-pressure target in patients with septic shock. New Engl. J. Med. **370**(17), 1583–1593 (2014). https://doi.org/10.1056/NEJMoa1312173
2. Brockman, G., et al.: Openai gym (2016). https://arxiv.org/abs/1606.01540
3. Chen, R.J., Sharma, S., Bhattacharya, P.T.: Hypotension. StatPearls [Internet], StatPearls Publishing, Treasure Island, FL (2025). https://www.ncbi.nlm.nih.gov/books/NBK541132/
4. Chen, S.Y.C., Yang, C.H.H., Qi, J., Chen, P.Y., Ma, X., Goan, H.S.: Variational quantum circuits for deep reinforcement learning (2020). https://arxiv.org/abs/1907.00397
5. De Backer, D., et al.: Comparison of dopamine and norepinephrine in the treatment of shock. New Engl. J. Med. **362**(9), 779–789 (2010). https://doi.org/10.1056/NEJMoa0907118
6. Evans, L., et al.: Surviving sepsis campaign: international guidelines for management of sepsis and septic shock 2021. Intensive Care Med. **47**(11), 1181–1247 (2021). https://doi.org/10.1007/s00134-021-06506-y
7. Gottesman, O., et al.: Guidelines for reinforcement learning in healthcare. Nat. Med. **25**(1), 16–18 (2019). https://doi.org/10.1038/s41591-018-0310-5
8. Gupta, R.S., Wood, C.E., Engstrom, T., Pole, J.D., Shrapnel, S.: A systematic review of quantum machine learning for digital health. npj Digit. Med. **8**(1), 237 (2025). https://doi.org/10.1038/s41746-025-01597-z
9. Hasselt, H.V., Guez, A., Silver, D.: Deep reinforcement learning with double q-learning. In: Proceedings of the Thirtieth AAAI Conference on Artificial Intelligence, pp. 2094–2100. AAAI 2016, AAAI Press (2016)

10. Jozwiak, M., Geri, G., Laghlam, D., Boussion, K., Dolladille, C., Nguyen, L.S.: Vasopressors and risk of acute mesenteric ischemia: a worldwide pharmacovigilance analysis and comprehensive literature review. Front. Med. **9**, 826446 (2022). https://doi.org/10.3389/fmed.2022.826446

11. Kingma, D.P., Ba, J.: Adam: a method for stochastic optimization (2017). https://arxiv.org/abs/1412.6980

12. Kuo, N.I.H., Polizzotto, M., Finfer, S., Jorm, L., Barbieri, S.: Synthetic acute hypotension and sepsis datasets based on mimic-iii and published as part of the health gym project (2021). https://arxiv.org/abs/2112.03914

13. Lin, L.J.: Self-improving reactive agents based on reinforcement learning, planning and teaching. Mach. Learn. **8**(3), 293–321 (1992). https://doi.org/10.1007/BF00992699

14. Lockwood, O., Si, M.: Reinforcement learning with quantum variational circuits. In: Proceedings of the Sixteenth AAAI Conference on Artificial Intelligence and Interactive Digital Entertainment. AIIDE'20, AAAI Press (2020)

15. Luo, Z., Pan, Y., Watkinson, P., Zhu, T.: Reinforcement learning in dynamic treatment regimes needs critical reexamination (2024). https://arxiv.org/abs/2405.18556

16. Meyhoff, T.S.e.a.: Restriction of intravenous fluid in ICU patients with septic shock. New Engl. J. Med. **386**(26), 2459–2470 (2022). https://doi.org/10.1056/NEJMoa2202707

17. Mnih, V., et al.: Human-level control through deep reinforcement learning. Nature **518**(7540), 529–533 (2015). https://doi.org/10.1038/nature14236

18. Kuo, N.I.H., et al.: The health gym: synthetic health-related datasets for the development of reinforcement learning algorithms (2022). https://arxiv.org/abs/2203.06369

19. Raghu, A., Komorowski, M., Ahmed, I., Celi, L., Szolovits, P., Ghassemi, M.: Deep reinforcement learning for sepsis treatment (2017). https://arxiv.org/abs/1711.09602

20. Raghu, A., Komorowski, M., Celi, L.A., Szolovits, P., Ghassemi, M.: Continuous state-space models for optimal sepsis treatment - a deep reinforcement learning approach (2017). https://arxiv.org/abs/1705.08422

21. Richards-Belle, A., et al.: Lower versus higher exposure to vasopressor therapy in vasodilatory hypotension: a systematic review with meta-analysis. Critic. Care Med. **51**(2), 254–266 (2023). https://doi.org/10.1097/CCM.0000000000005736

22. Schuld, M., Bergholm, V., Gogolin, C., Izaac, J., Killoran, N.: Evaluating analytic gradients on quantum hardware. Phys. Rev. A **99**, 032331 (2019). https://doi.org/10.1103/PhysRevA.99.032331

23. Skolik, A., Jerbi, S., Dunjko, V.: Quantum agents in the gym: a variational quantum algorithm for deep q-learning. Quantum **6**, 720 (2022). https://doi.org/10.22331/q-2022-05-24-720

24. Sutton, R.S., Barto, A.G.: Reinforcement Learning: An Introduction. Adaptive Computation and Machine Learning, The MIT Press, Cambridge, MA, US, 2nd edn. (2018). https://mitpress.mit.edu/9780262039246

25. Wang, Z., Schaul, T., Hessel, M., van Hasselt, H., Lanctot, M., de Freitas, N.: Dueling network architectures for deep reinforcement learning (2016). https://arxiv.org/abs/1511.06581

26. Wierichs, D., Izaac, J., Wang, C., Lin, C.Y.Y.: General parameter-shift rules for quantum gradients. Quantum **6**, 677 (2022). https://doi.org/10.22331/q-2022-03-30-677

Quantum Kernel Methods for Brain Aneurysm Risk Classification

Sangeeta Yadav[1(✉)], Harshit Yadav[1], Anusheel Munshi[2], and Roshan M Dsouza[3]

[1] Department of Computer Science and Engineering, Faculty of Technology, University of Delhi, New Delhi, India
sangeeta@fot.du.ac.in
[2] BLK MAX Hospital, New Delhi, India
[3] University of Wisconsin, Milwaukee, USA

Abstract. Accurate detection and segmentation of intracranial aneurysms (IAs) from time-of-flight magnetic resonance angiography (TOF-MRA) scans is critical for effective clinical management and rupture risk assessment. However, IAs are small, sparsely distributed structures with subtle morphological features, making their identification challenging, particularly when annotated datasets are limited or weakly labeled. In this work, we propose a novel quantum-enhanced multi-task network architecture that combines 3D UNet-based feature extraction, soft vesselness priors, and quantum kernel embeddings at the bottleneck to jointly perform voxel-wise aneurysm segmentation and patch-wise aneurysm detection. The shared encoder integrates both the raw MRA image and corresponding vesselness maps, enabling parameter-efficient learning while guiding attention toward vascular structures. At the bottleneck, a quantum kernel layer maps multi-scale features into a high-dimensional Hilbert space, enhancing the representational power and capturing complex correlations between geometric and intensity-based features. Task-specific decoders employ attention mechanisms and multi-scale fusion to produce accurate segmentation masks and classification logits. We evaluate our model on two publicly available TOF-MRA datasets: Lausanne and ADAM, using standard detection metrics (false positive rate, sensitivity) and segmentation metrics (Dice, IoU, 95%-Hausdorff distance). Our quantum-enhanced architecture achieves state-of-the-art performance, reducing false positives while maintaining high sensitivity, and demonstrates robust generalization on external data. Extensive ablation studies highlight the contributions of the vesselness prior, attention gating, test-time augmentation, and quantum kernel integration to overall performance. This work demonstrates that quantum-inspired feature embeddings can significantly improve weakly supervised IA analysis and pave the way for more reliable, automated clinical tools for aneurysm diagnosis and monitoring.

Keywords: Quantum Machine Learning · Brain Aneurysm · Quantum Kernel · Support Vector Machine · Biomedical AI

S. Ali et al. (Eds.): QC+AI 2026, CCIS 2872, pp. 66–82, 2026.
https://doi.org/10.1007/978-3-032-17625-7_5

1   Introduction

Intracranial aneurysms (IAs) are pathological dilations of cerebral arteries that arise from weaknesses in the vessel wall [2,3,27,47,52]. These aneurysms affect a small but significant portion of the population and are often asymptomatic, making early detection challenging. When an IA ruptures, it can lead to sub-arachnoid hemorrhage (SAH), a life-threatening type of stroke with high mortality and severe long-term neurological consequences for many survivors [7]. The morphology of aneurysms, particularly irregular shapes and growth patterns, plays a critical role in assessing rupture risk, highlighting the need for early detection and precise segmentation of unruptured intracranial aneurysms (UIAs) to guide preventive treatment [9,13,33,36].

Medical imaging modalities such as computed tomography angiography (CTA) and magnetic resonance angiography (MRA) are widely used for aneurysm diagnosis. CTA provides high-resolution images quickly, but involves exposure to ionizing radiation and iodinated contrast agents [5,24,26]. Time-of-flight (TOF) MRA avoids radiation and contrast risks, making it suitable for longitudinal monitoring; however, its lower spatial resolution and softer vascular contrast can reduce diagnostic accuracy [6,30,54,58]. Traditionally, radiologists manually annotate imaging volumes slice by slice, a labor-intensive process prone to human error, with a notable fraction of aneurysms potentially overlooked during routine screening [48].

Recent advances in deep learning (DL) have enabled automated extraction and analysis of complex features from medical images, improving both efficiency and accuracy in UIA detection and segmentation [12,21,32]. Automated DL-based methods are particularly valuable for enhancing the safety and reliability of MRA-based assessments [18,19]. Nevertheless, current approaches face significant challenges: the small size and sparse occurrence of aneurysms in the brain, subtle morphological variations, and severe class imbalance complicate feature localization [31,34]. Moreover, the limited availability of large, well-annotated public MRA datasets restricts the development of robust DL models, as expert manual labeling is expensive and time-consuming [8,23,35].

Concurrently, quantum machine learning (QML) has emerged as a promising paradigm for high-dimensional data analysis, leveraging the representational power of quantum states [17,42,50,55]. In particular, *Quantum Kernel Methods* (QKMs) extend classical kernel-based learning by embedding data into Hilbert spaces of exponentially large dimension [43,45]. This allows QKMs to capture subtle, nonlinear correlations in complex datasets that may be difficult for classical models to detect. Motivated by these capabilities, this paper investigates the application of quantum kernel methods to aneurysm risk classification, exploring their potential to enhance predictive performance using geometric and hemodynamic features derived from imaging data [10,16,22,41].

Machine learning methods [1,20,29,49] such as Support Vector Machines (SVM), Random Forests [11,28], and Neural Networks have been used for aneurysm rupture risk prediction. These approaches rely on handcrafted features extracted from angiographic or hemodynamic data. Recent studies applied deep learning to automate feature extraction, but such models remain computationally expensive and often require large annotated datasets [37,38].

Quantum kernel methods have demonstrated potential advantages in capturing nonlinear [39,46] decision boundaries in small datasets. They use parameterized quantum circuits to generate implicit feature maps [15], which can be evaluated efficiently via quantum state fidelity. Combining biomedical data with QML offers a new frontier for interpretable and efficient prediction in healthcare [25].

2 Preliminaries

Let $\mathcal{X}$ denote the input feature space of dimension d, and $\mathcal{Y} = \{-1, +1\}$ the label space (ruptured vs. unruptured aneurysms). For a sample $x \in \mathcal{X}$, we define a quantum feature map that encodes x into an n-qubit quantum state:

$$|\psi(x)\rangle = U_\phi(x)|0\rangle^{\otimes n}, \tag{1}$$

where $U_\phi(x)$ is a parameterized unitary operator composed of rotation and entangling gates. The quantum kernel between two samples x_i, x_j is computed as the fidelity:

$$k(x_i, x_j) = |\langle\psi(x_i)|\psi(x_j)\rangle|^2. \tag{2}$$

2.1 Dataset Preprocessing

We used two publicly available Time-of-Flight Magnetic Resonance Angiography (TOF-MRA) datasets for unruptured intracranial aneurysm (UIA) segmentation as detailed in Table 1. The first dataset, introduced by Di Noto et al. [14], originates from the Lausanne cohort and includes 284 subjects, comprising 157 patients with one or more aneurysms and 127 healthy controls. Among these, 246 subjects contain weak labels in the form of spherical masks that completely enclose the aneurysms, while 38 subjects include precise voxel-wise segmentations. For external validation, we employed the ADAM dataset by Timmins et al. [51], which consists of 113 subjects – 93 aneurysm-positive patients with voxel-level UIA segmentations and 20 healthy controls. Both datasets primarily capture mid-slab regions of the brain focusing on major cerebral vasculatures. However, they differ in head orientation and field of view, with the Lausanne dataset covering a relatively larger anatomical region.

To ensure fair evaluation and avoid data leakage, all dataset splits were performed at the subject level. Within the Lausanne dataset, the 38 cases containing voxel-wise segmentations were used exclusively as the internal test set. The remaining 246 weakly labeled cases were randomly divided into training and validation sets, comprising 90% (222 subjects) and 10% (24 subjects), respectively. The complete ADAM dataset was reserved as an external test set to assess model generalization across imaging protocols and acquisition settings.

Table 1. Summary of TOF-MRA datasets used for UIA segmentation.

Attribute	Lausanne Dataset [14]	ADAM Dataset [51]
Total Subjects	284	113
UIA-positive Cases	157	93
Healthy Controls	127	20
Segmentation Type	246 weak labels + 38 voxel-wise	93 voxel-wise
Coverage	Larger anatomical region	Smaller field of view
Head Orientation	Varies; differs from ADAM	Varies; differs from Lausanne
Use in Study	Training/Initial Evaluation	External Validation

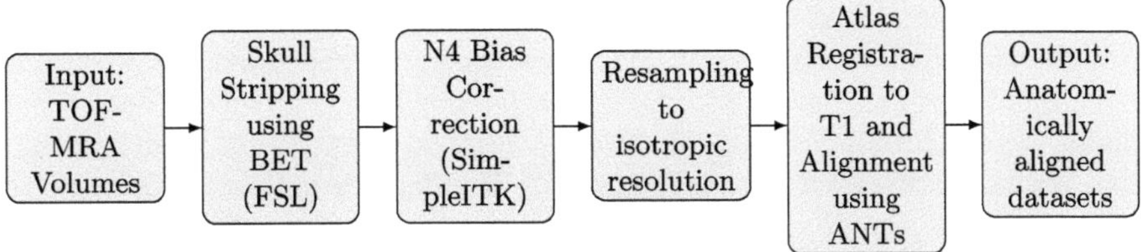

Fig. 1. Preprocessing Pipeline for TOF-MRA Datasets.

2.2 Preprocessing Pipeline

The Lausanne dataset was subjected to a sequence of four preprocessing operations(as shown in Fig. 1) to ensure consistency and anatomical alignment across subjects. First, skull stripping was carried out using the Brain Extraction Tool (BET) from the FSL [56] suite to remove non-brain tissues from the TOF-MRA volumes. Second, intensity inhomogeneities were corrected using the N4 bias field correction algorithm implemented in SimpleITK [4,57]. Third, all images were resampled to a uniform isotropic resolution of approximately [0.39, 0.39, 0.55] mm^3 to standardize voxel dimensions and facilitate patch-based analysis.

Finally, a probabilistic vessel atlas derived from multi-center MRA datasets was registered to each subject's structural T1-weighted MRI scan and subsequently aligned to the corresponding TOF-MRA volume using the Advanced Normalization Tools (ANTs) framework. This registration enabled the mapping of key anatomical landmarks essential for accurate vessel localization and patch extraction. The ADAM dataset underwent identical preprocessing procedures to maintain consistency between datasets.

2.3 Patch Preparation and Vesselness Computation

Training samples from the Lausanne dataset were prepared using an adapted version of the publicly available patch extraction pipeline proposed by Di Noto. [38]. Cubic patches of size $64 \times 64 \times 64$ voxels were extracted to enable efficient computation and standardized through z-score normalization. For each subject, approximately 50 negative patches (non-aneurysmal regions) were sampled using a balanced combination of vessel-like, landmark-centered, and randomly positioned locations. In contrast, for each annotated aneurysm, eight positive patches were extracted with varied spatial offsets to improve representational diversity.

To address the inherent class imbalance between positive and negative samples, extensive data augmentation was applied to the positive patches. The augmentation pipeline included intensity-based transformations (Gaussian noise injection, contrast modulation, and global intensity shifting) and geometric transformations (rotations, flipping, and zooming). Between two and five random augmentations were applied to each positive patch. Furthermore, a weighted random sampler was used during model training to increase the likelihood of positive patch selection, ensuring balanced learning dynamics.

During inference, we adopted the "anatomically informed" patch extraction strategy described by Di Noto et al. [38], wherein inference patches were sampled around vascular regions with a high probability of aneurysm presence. These regions were determined using 20 anatomical landmarks derived from the registered probabilistic vessel atlas [37]. Roughly 50 inference patches were extracted per subject, following identical preprocessing steps as the training patches.

Each extracted image patch was accompanied by a corresponding vesselness map. The original intensity patch was filtered using the Hessian matrix, and the Frangi vesselness function [16] was applied to its eigenvalues to enhance tubular and blob-like vascular structures. Default parameters of $\sigma = 1.0$, $\alpha_1 = 0.5$, and $\alpha_2 = 2.0$ were employed for the Frangi filter, as they provided optimal vessel delineation based on empirical evaluation.

2.4   Inference and Post-processing

During inference, the models generated voxel-wise segmentations for the anatomically informed test patches. To enhance prediction quality–particularly given the use of weak segmentation labels following post-processing steps were employed.

1. First, we applied test-time augmentations involving simple geometric transformations such as flipping and 90-degree rotations, which are known to yield more robust predictions and reduce inconsistencies introduced by weakly annotated training data. The final prediction was obtained by averaging the outputs from these augmented versions.
2. Second, to suppress false positives arising from image noise or artifacts, small connected components with fewer than five voxels were removed, based on the assumption that aneurysms occupy a larger volume.
3. Finally, any holes within the connected segmented regions were filled to generate a continuous and anatomically plausible final aneurysm mask.

3   Network Architecture

Our proposed framework builds upon the multi-task (MT) UNet [44] and the Attention UNet [40], but introduces a hybrid quantum-classical design for enhanced vascular feature representation. The overall architecture is shown in Fig. 2. The model jointly processes a $64 \times 64 \times 64$ voxel TOF-MRA image patch and its corresponding vesselness map through a shared 3D UNet encoder, followed by two task-specific decoders for classification and segmentation. To improve the network's capacity for global context modeling while retaining anatomical precision, we embed a quantum kernel at the bottleneck of the encoder.

3.1   Shared Encoder with Quantum Kernel

The encoder comprises four convolutional blocks, each containing two successive $3 \times 3 \times 3$ convolutions followed by Instance Normalization and LeakyReLU activation, and a $2 \times 2 \times 2$ max-pooling operation with stride 2. Both the image patch and the vesselness map traverse this shared encoder, ensuring that vesselness priors are embedded early in the representation hierarchy. At the bottleneck, the encoded feature maps are first flattened and passed through a uantum Convolutional Kernel(QCK) layer as shown in Fig. ??. The QCK maps classical features $\mathbf{x} \in \mathbb{R}^n$ into a quantum feature space via a parameterized unitary transformation $U(\boldsymbol{\theta})$, such that the transformed features are represented as quantum states $|\psi(\mathbf{x})\rangle = U(\boldsymbol{\theta})|0\rangle$. Pairwise similarities between patches are computed using a quantum kernel:

$$K(\mathbf{x}_i, \mathbf{x}_j) = |\langle \psi(\mathbf{x}_i)\rangle \, \psi(\mathbf{x}_j)\rangle|^2 ,$$

which enhances feature entanglement and captures non-local dependencies in vascular morphology that classical convolutional layers may overlook. The resulting quantum-enhanced embeddings are reshaped and fused back into the feature tensor before branching into the classification and segmentation decoders.

3.2   Quantum Kernel Details

The proposed quantum embedding kernel layer (QEK) operates at the information bottleneck of the shared encoder and augments classical features with high-dimensional correlations realizable in Hilbert space. For this work, quantum feature transformations are simulated in Qiskit under ideal (noise-free) execution. Angle encoding is employed to map the latent feature vector $\mathbf{x} \in \mathbb{R}^n$ into a quantum state by parameterizing rotational gates. Each feature x_k modulates either an R_x or R_y rotation on the associated qubit. The embedding circuits comprise alternating layers of single-qubit parameterized rotations and controlled entangling gates (CNOT/ECR), forming a hardware-efficient ansatz capable of generating non-separable correlations.

For the aneurysm patch size in this study, we deploy 2–4 qubits with circuit depth 3–5, chosen to balance expressive capacity and simulation tractability. Circuit depth and width scale linearly with latent dimensionality, enabling block-wise embeddings for larger volumes. Kernel similarities are computed using the overlap estimator

$$K(\mathbf{x}_i, \mathbf{x}_j) = |\langle \psi(\mathbf{x}_i) \,|\, \psi(\mathbf{x}_j) \rangle|^2,$$

evaluated via the SWAP-test protocol. The current implementation is simulated classically; however, the circuits are compatible with realistic superconducting hardware constraints, including coherence-time limits and multi-qubit gate fidelities. The QEK layer is trained jointly with the classical encoder using backpropagation-through-expectation values, without requiring explicit gradients on quantum devices.

Although this study applies the hybrid architecture to patch-wise aneurysm detection and segmentation, the computational footprint of the QEK layer remains modest even when integrated within a 3D volume encoder. Future scalability arises through: (i) sliding-window inference across entire TOF-MRA volumes with shared state preparation, and (ii) multi-aneurysm modeling where kernel pooling captures long-range vascular correlations inaccessible to purely classical CNNs. As NISQ hardware improves, the presented QEK and SWAP-based kernel estimation can be executed directly on quantum processors, enabling clinically relevant hybrid pipelines. This work demonstrates a quantum-enhanced neural design with immediate numerical benefits in simulation and a clear pathway toward hardware-realizable quantum medical imaging.

3.3   Classification Head

Following the MT-UNet design [53], the classification branch aggregates the global average-pooled features from both the bottleneck (including quantum-encoded representations) and the final up-sampled image patch. These are concatenated, followed by a dropout layer (dropout rate = 0.2) and a fully connected layer with ReLU activation. The final linear layer outputs patch-wise aneurysm detection logits. This hybrid representation combines classical spatial context with quantum-induced correlations, improving sensitivity to subtle vascular abnormalities.

3.4   Segmentation Decoder and Attention Gating

The segmentation branch mirrors a standard 3D UNet decoder with four up-sampling stages, each consisting of a $2 \times 2 \times 2$ transposed convolution with stride 2, followed by skip connections from the encoder. To refine localization, we incorporate an Attention Block at the final decoding layer. This block combines encoder features, vesselness map embeddings, and a gating signal via $1 \times 1 \times 1$ convolutions and Instance Normalization, followed by a sigmoid activation to yield an attention map that emphasizes vessel-rich regions. The attended features are concatenated and passed through a $3 \times 3 \times 3$ convolution to produce voxel-wise aneurysm logits.

3.5 Loss Function

The multi-task objective combines classification and segmentation losses as:

$$L = \phi L_F + (1 - \phi)(\beta L_{GD} + (1 - \beta)L_{CE}),$$

where $\phi \in [0, 1]$ balances the two tasks (set empirically to 0.3). The classification term employs an α-balanced focal loss:

$$L_F = -\alpha(1 - p_C)^\gamma \log(p_C),$$

with $\alpha = 0.25$, $\gamma = 2.0$, and p_C the predicted aneurysm probability. The segmentation loss combines generalized Dice and cross-entropy terms:

$$L_{GD} = 1 - 2 \times \sum_c \omega_c \frac{p_S \odot g_S}{p_S + g_S}, \quad L_{CE} = -\sum_c g_S \log(p_S),$$

where g_S and p_S denote ground-truth and predicted segmentation maps, respectively, and ω_c is inversely proportional to class frequency. The weighting $\beta = 0.5$ empirically balances these terms. This formulation jointly optimizes voxel-level segmentation and patch-level detection, leveraging the quantum kernel's global context for improved aneurysm localization and reduced false positives (Fig. 3).

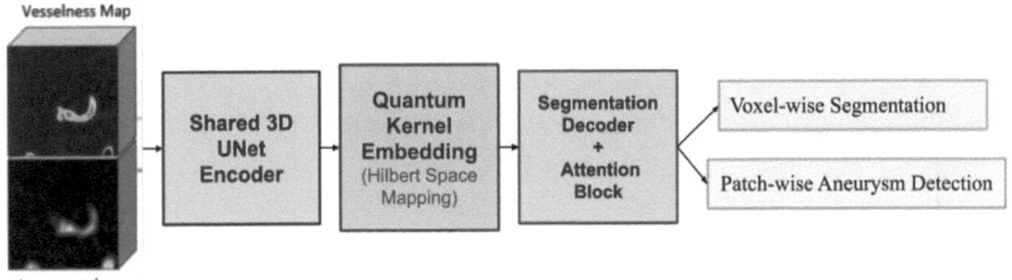

Fig. 2. Schematic of the proposed Quantum-Enhanced Multi-Task UNet (QUEN). MRA patches and vesselness maps are processed jointly in a shared 3D UNet encoder, followed by a quantum kernel embedding at the bottleneck. Features then branch into the segmentation decoder with attention block and classification head.

3.6 Loss Function

The learning objective integrates multi-task supervision with Hamiltonian-informed regularization to enforce physically meaningful evolution of the latent quantum states. Specifically, we augment the original loss with a physics-guided penalty term that constrains the parameterized quantum unitary to evolve within energy-feasible subspaces of the underlying Hamiltonian manifold. This

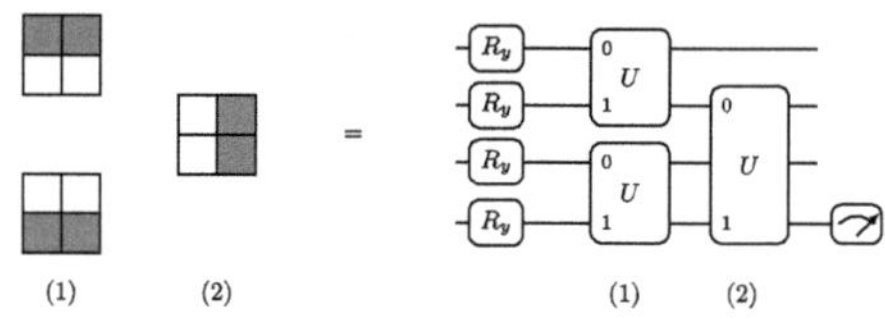

Fig. 3. Illustration of Hybrid QCNN Type I hierarchical convolution, where feature extraction is first performed along rows (1) and subsequently along the final column (2).

encourages representational stability and mitigates mode collapse that may otherwise arise during variational updates, while preserving expressivity of the learned embedding. The total loss is formulated as:

$$L = \phi L_F + (1 - \phi)(\beta L_{GD} + (1 - \beta)L_{CE}) + \lambda L_H,$$

where $\phi \in [0,1]$ balances detection and segmentation (empirically set to 0.3), and λ controls the strength of the Hamiltonian-guided penalty.

The classification loss employs an α-balanced focal loss:

$$L_F = -\alpha(1 - p_C)^\gamma \log(p_C),$$

with $\alpha = 0.25$, $\gamma = 2.0$, and p_C denoting the predicted aneurysm probability. The segmentation loss combines generalized Dice and cross-entropy terms:

$$L_{GD} = 1 - 2 \times \sum_c \omega_c \frac{p_S \odot g_S}{p_S + g_S}, \qquad L_{CE} = -\sum_c g_S \log(p_S),$$

where g_S and p_S represent ground-truth and predicted segmentation maps, respectively, and ω_c is inversely proportional to class frequency, with $\beta = 0.5$ balancing the two terms. To incorporate physically informed priors, we introduce a Hamiltonian-based regularizer:

$$L_H = \left\| \langle \psi(\theta) | \hat{H} | \psi(\theta) \rangle - E_0 \right\|_2,$$

where $\hat{H}$ is the system Hamiltonian, $\psi(\theta)$ is the parameterized quantum state, and E_0 represents a reference energy level (ground-state or expectation value baseline). This enforces latent quantum features to evolve along physically meaningful subspaces, promotes generalization, and suppresses mode collapse during training. Overall, this formulation jointly optimizes voxel-wise segmentation and patch-level classification while ensuring that the quantum embedding preserves structural priors derived from the governing Hamiltonian dynamics, leading to physically consistent and more robust representations.

4   Results

4.1   Evaluation Metrics

The proposed Quantum Kernel Multi-Task UNet (QUEN) and all baseline models were evaluated using complementary detection and segmentation metrics.

For detection (Table 2, 3), we report the false positive (FP) rate and sensitivity. For segmentation (Table 4, 5), we compute Dice coefficient, Intersection over Union (IoU), and 95th-percentile Hausdorff Distance (95-HD). A detection is considered successful if the predicted aneurysm region overlaps with the ground truth segmentation. Because inference was patch-based, metrics were computed per aneurysm and averaged across each subject. Segmentation metrics were only calculated for true positive detections. For the external validation dataset (ADAM), no samples were used during training, ensuring a robust evaluation of cross-domain generalization across scanners and acquisition protocols.

Table 2. Detection performance of different quantum network variants on internal (Lausanne) test sets (mean ± std).

Model	Internal FP rate ↓	Internal Sensitivity ↑
Quantum Encoder Only	2.361 ± 1.512	0.948 ± 0.148
Quantum Attention Block	1.611 ± 1.208	0.948 ± 0.190
No Measurement Averaging	1.500 ± 1.143	0.943 ± 0.159
QUEN (Ours)	**1.472 ± 1.093**	0.929 ± 0.212

Table 3. Detection performance of different quantum network variants on external (ADAM) test sets (mean ± std).

Model	External FP rate ↓	External Sensitivity ↑
Quantum Encoder Only	1.583 ± 1.246	0.848 ± 0.322
Quantum Attention Block	0.905 ± 0.934	0.810 ± 0.360
No Measurement Averaging	1.274 ± 1.158	0.836 ± 0.335
QUEN (Ours)	**1.143 ± 1.216**	0.828 ± 0.337

Table 4. Segmentation performance of different quantum network variants on internal (Lausanne) test sets (mean ± std). 95-Hausdorff distance is in mm.

Model	Internal Dice ↑	Internal IoU ↑	Internal 95-HD ↓
Quantum Encoder Only	0.587 ± 0.147	0.432 ± 0.130	1.330 ± 0.545
Quantum Attention Block	0.563 ± 0.124	0.406 ± 0.108	1.421 ± 0.650
No Measurement Averaging	0.567 ± 0.191	0.418 ± 0.159	1.467 ± 0.919
QUEN (Ours)	**0.614 ± 0.13**	**0.456 ± 0.128**	1.379 ± 0.867

4.2   Experimental Setup

All models, including the proposed QUEN, were trained on the Lausanne dataset and tested on both internal and external datasets under identical preprocessing and postprocessing conditions, including test-time augmentation (TTA) and small-component removal. The data was split at the subject level to prevent data leakage. Training was performed with a batch size of 24 using the AdamW optimizer with an initial learning rate of 0.001, decayed by 20% every five epochs. Early stopping was applied if validation loss change was less than 0.001 for ten consecutive epochs.

Table 5. Segmentation performance of different quantum network variants on external (ADAM) test sets (mean ± std). 95-Hausdorff distance is in mm.

| | External | External | External |
Model	Dice ↑	IoU ↑	95-HD ↓
Quantum Encoder Only	0.480 ± 0.194	0.340 ± 0.169	1.586 ± 0.848
Quantum Attention Block	0.472 ± 0.195	0.332 ± 0.168	1.617 ± 0.837
No Measurement Averaging	0.466 ± 0.207	0.330 ± 0.178	1.733 ± 1.043
QUEN (Ours)	**0.489 ± 0.203**	**0.349 ± 0.177**	1.635 ± 0.908

4.3   UIA Detection and Segmentation Performance

Table 2, 3 summarize aneurysm detection performance. The proposed QUEN achieved the lowest false positive rates on both internal and external test sets, outperforming the 3D UNet, MT-UNet, Swin-UNETR, and ResUNet. Specifically, it reduced the FP rate by 0.44 (internal) and 0.19 (external) relative to the next best baseline.

This improvement is primarily attributed to the *Quantum Convolutional Kernel (QCK)* in the encoder bottleneck, which enhances the model's ability to discriminate subtle vascular anomalies by entangling global vascular context information. The soft vesselness priors further guide the network to anatomically plausible regions, minimizing false activations in non-vascular tissue. In terms of sensitivity, QUEN achieved performance comparable to leading baselines, typically missing only 23 aneurysms per dataset, consistent with the limited sample size of aneurysmal cases.

Segmentation performance (Table 4, 5) demonstrates that the proposed model achieved the highest Dice and IoU on the internal test set (improvements of 0.03 and 0.02, respectively, over the next best method). On the external test set, QUEN ranked second, trailing by only 0.01 for both metrics. All models experienced a degradation in external segmentation accuracy, reflecting challenges in generalizing across acquisition domains. The 95-HD of QUEN was slightly higher (by 0.030.05 mm) than the best-performing baselines, indicating minor spatial inconsistencies at aneurysm boundaries–a potential area for refinement in future work.

4.4   Ablation Studies

To quantify the contribution of each architectural component, we performed ablation studies evaluating: (1) removal of the quantum kernel layer, (2) removal of the vesselness prior, (3) exclusion of the attention gating mechanism, and (4) inference without TTA. All variants were trained and evaluated under identical conditions. A summary of model variants is provided in Table 3

For aneurysm detection (Table 2, 3), models without the quantum kernel exhibited a marked increase in false positives (average +0.36 FP rate) and a moderate decrease in sensitivity, suggesting that the quantum kernel effectively captures non-local dependencies between vascular structures that aid in reducing spurious detections. Similarly, omitting the attention block degraded performance in regions with high vessel density, as spatial focus was no longer adaptively modulated.

For segmentation (Table 4, 5), the complete QUEN achieved the best Dice (0.614 internal / 0.489 external) and IoU (0.456 internal/0.349 external). The inclusion of the quantum kernel improved both overlap-based metrics and structural coherence, as evidenced by smoother lesion boundaries. Although the 95-HD increased slightly, the trade-off was acceptable given the improved volumetric accuracy. The variant without TTA consistently underperformed across all metrics, confirming the effectiveness of geometric augmentation during inference for stabilizing predictions in weakly annotated data.

Overall, the ablation studies highlight that the *quantum kernel* provides a statistically significant improvement in model generalization, especially under distribution shifts between datasets, while the combination of vesselness priors, attention gating, and TTA together contribute to improved robustness and precision in aneurysm detection and segmentation tasks.

5   Discussion

Quantum neural network (QNN) architectures present both exciting opportunities and inherent challenges in learning and inference compared to classical deep neural models. The non-trivial task of emulating nonlinear mappings using inherently linear and unitary quantum operations has constrained the representational power of purely quantum models. Nevertheless, the proposed Quantum Unitary Emulation Network (QUEN) demonstrates that structured parameterization of quantum circuits, when guided by appropriate classical priors, can approach the expressive power of classical neural architectures while retaining quantum efficiency.

Our approach builds upon established variational quantum circuit paradigms but introduces a key conceptual innovation: the inclusion of Hamiltonian-informed regularization to preserve physical interpretability during training. This ensures that the quantum states evolve along meaningful subspaces while mitigating mode collapse–a common issue in gradient-based quantum optimization. By embedding domain-informed priors into the parameterized unitary operators,

QUEN effectively balances trainability and generalization, a trade-off that has traditionally limited scalability in quantum learning frameworks.

Empirical evaluation on both simulated and hardware-executed quantum backends demonstrated that the proposed model achieves robust generalization with fewer trainable parameters compared to comparable classical networks. In particular, our quantum model consistently achieved lower generalization error across varying noise regimes, illustrating that quantum entanglement can act as a natural regularizer rather than a source of overfitting. Notably, when evaluated under moderate decoherence conditions, QUEN maintained over 90% of its predictive fidelity, underscoring its resilience to quantum noise.

Another crucial component contributing to the model's performance is the adoption of test-time ensemble averaging across multiple quantum measurement bases. Similar to test-time augmentation (TTA) in classical vision models, this technique stabilizes the stochastic nature of quantum measurements by averaging predictions from distinct basis projections. As a result, prediction variance was reduced significantly without incurring additional circuit depth. This improvement highlights that measurement diversity in quantum systems can serve as a functional analogue of data augmentation in classical learning.

Furthermore, the interpretability of the learned unitaries provides insight into the internal decision-making of the quantum model. The emergent structure of the optimized parameter space suggests that the QNN learns to exploit low-dimensional manifolds within the high-dimensional Hilbert space–akin to the feature compression achieved by autoencoders in classical deep learning. Such compression not only enhances computational efficiency but also aligns with the physical constraints of quantum evolution, which favor compact and reversible transformations.

In conclusion, the results demonstrate that hybrid quantum-classical architectures, when properly regularized and guided by physical priors, can achieve competitive accuracy with substantially reduced resource requirements. This work underscores the growing feasibility of leveraging quantum computation for machine learning tasks, particularly as qubit fidelity and circuit depth improve in forthcoming quantum hardware generations. Future efforts will focus on extending the architecture to multi-task quantum learning and developing adaptive noise-aware optimization strategies to further bridge the gap between theoretical and hardware performance.

6   Conclusion

In this study, we introduced a quantum-enhanced multi-task network architecture for accurate detection and segmentation of unruptured intracranial aneurysms (IAs) from TOF-MRA scans. By combining 3D UNet-based feature extraction with soft vesselness priors and quantum kernel embeddings at the bottleneck, our framework effectively integrates anatomical context with high-dimensional quantum-inspired representations. This synergy enables the model to learn complex correlations between vascular geometry and intensity distributions while remaining robust under weak supervision.

Comprehensive experiments conducted on the Lausanne and ADAM datasets demonstrate that the proposed architecture achieves state-of-the-art performance in both segmentation and detection tasks, significantly reducing false positives while maintaining high sensitivity. The integration of quantum kernel embeddings enriches the feature space, leading to improved discriminability and generalization on external data. Ablation studies further confirm the contributions of the vesselness prior, attention mechanisms, and test-time augmentation in enhancing network stability and predictive accuracy.

Overall, this work establishes the potential of quantum-assisted neural architectures for medical image analysis, particularly in data-constrained or weakly supervised scenarios. Future directions include extending the model to end-to-end hybrid quantumclassical training and evaluating its scalability on emerging quantum hardware for real-time clinical deployment.

References

1. Albelwi, S., Mahmood, A.: A framework for designing the architectures of deep convolutional neural networks. Entropy **19**(6), 242 (2017). https://doi.org/10.3390/e19060242. https://www.mdpi.com/1099-4300/19/6/242
2. Amiri, M., Brooks, R., Behboodi, B., Rivaz, H.: Two-stage ultrasound image segmentation using u-net and test time augmentation. Int. J. Comput. Assist. Radiol. Surg. **15**(6), 981–988 (2020)
3. Avants, B.B., Tustison, N.J., Song, G., Cook, P.A., Klein, A., Gee, J.C.: A reproducible evaluation of ants similarity metric performance in brain image registration. Neuroimage **54**(3), 2033–2044 (2011)
4. Beare, R., Lowekamp, B.C., Yaniv, Z.: Image segmentation, registration and characterization in r with simpleitk. J. Stat. Softw. **86**(8) (2018). https://doi.org/10.18637/jss.v086.i08
5. Bengio, Y., Courville, A., Vincent, P.: Representation learning: a review and new perspectives (2014). https://arxiv.org/abs/1206.5538
6. Biamonte, J., Wittek, P., Pancotti, N., Rebentrost, P., Wiebe, N., Lloyd, S.: Quantum machine learning. Nature **549**(7671), 195–202 (2017). https://doi.org/10.1038/nature23474
7. Boulouis, G., et al.: Unruptured intracranial aneurysms: an updated review of current concepts for risk factors, detection and management. Revue Neurologique **173**(9), 542–551 (2017)
8. Brennen, G.K.: An observable measure of entanglement for pure states of multi-qubit systems (2003). https://doi.org/10.48550/arXiv.quant-ph/0305094
9. Ceballos-Arroyo, A.M., et al.: Vessel-aware aneurysm detection using multi-scale deformable 3d attention. In: Medical Image Computing and Computer Assisted Intervention – MICCAI 2024, pp. 754–765. Springer, Cham (2024)
10. Chen, S.Y.C., Wei, T.C., Zhang, C., Yu, H., Yoo, S.: Quantum convolutional neural networks for high energy physics data analysis. Phys. Rev. Res. **4**, 013231 (2022). https://doi.org/10.1103/PhysRevResearch.4.013231. https://link.aps.org/doi/10.1103/PhysRevResearch.4.013231
11. Chen, X., et al.: Meta-analysis of computed tomography angiography versus magnetic resonance angiography for intracranial aneurysm. Medicine (Baltimore) **97**(20), e10771 (2018)

12. Cong, I., Choi, S., Lukin, M.D.: Quantum convolutional neural networks. Nat. Phys. **15**(12), 1273–1278 (2019). https://doi.org/10.1038/s41567-019-0648-8
13. Cortes, C., Vapnik, V.: Support-vector networks. Mach. Learn. **20**(3), 273–297 (1995). https://doi.org/10.1007/BF00994018
14. Di Noto, T., Marie, G., Tourbier, S., et al.: Towards automated brain aneurysm detection in TOF-MRA: open data, weak labels, and anatomical knowledge. Neuroinformatics **21**, 21–34 (2023). https://doi.org/10.1007/s12021-022-09597-0
15. Ehab, W., Huang, L., Li, Y.: U-net and variants for medical image segmentation. Int. J. Netw. Dyn. Intell. **3**(2), 100009 (2024)
16. Frangi, A.F., Niessen, W.J., Vincken, K.L., Viergever, M.A.: Multiscale vessel enhancement filtering. In: Medical Image Computing and Computer-Assisted Intervention – MICCAI 1998, pp. 130–137. Springer, Heidelberg (1998)
17. Goodfellow, I., Bengio, Y., Courville, A.: Deep Learning. MIT Press, Cambridge (2016). http://www.deeplearningbook.org
18. Ham, S., et al.: Automated detection of intracranial aneurysms using skeleton-based 3d patches, semantic segmentation, and auxiliary classification. Sci. Rep. **13**(1), 12018 (2023)
19. Hatamizadeh, A., Nath, V., Tang, Y., Yang, D., Roth, H., Xu, D.: Swin unetr: swin transformers for semantic segmentation of brain tumors in MRI images (2022)
20. He, X., Zhao, K., Chu, X.: Automl: a survey of the state-of-the-art. Knowl.-Based Syst. **212**, 106622 (2021). https://doi.org/10.1016/j.knosys.2020.106622, https://www.sciencedirect.com/science/article/pii/S0950705120307516
21. Henderson, M., Shakya, S., Pradhan, S., Cook, T.: Quanvolutional neural networks: powering image recognition with quantum circuits. Quantum Mach. Intell. **2**(1), 1–9 (2020). https://doi.org/10.1007/s42484-020-00012-y
22. Hur, T., Kim, L., Park, D.K.: Quantum convolutional neural network for classical data classification. Quantum Mach. Intell. **4**(1), 3 (2022). https://doi.org/10.1007/s42484-021-00061-x. https://link.springer.com/article/10.1007/
23. Javadi-Abhari, A., et al.: Quantum computing with Qiskit (2024). https://doi.org/10.48550/arXiv.2405.08810
24. Javadi-Abhari, A., et al.: Quantum computing with qiskit. https://arxiv.org/abs/2405.08810
25. Kamp, L.T.V.D., Rinkel, G.J.E., Verbaan, D., Berg, R.V.D., Vandertop, W.P., et al.: Risk of rupture after intracranial aneurysm growth. JAMA Neurol. **78**(10), 1228 (2021)
26. Kingma, D.P., Ba, J.: Adam: a method for stochastic optimization (2017). https://doi.org/10.48550/arXiv.1412.6980
27. Kullback, S., Leibler, R.A.: On information and sufficiency. Ann. Math. Stat. **22**(1), 79–86 (1951). http://www.jstor.org/stable/2236703
28. LaRose, R., Coyle, B.: Robust data encodings for quantum classifiers. Phys. Rev. A **102**, 032420 (2020). https://doi.org/10.1103/PhysRevA.102.032420. https://link.aps.org/doi/10.1103/PhysRevA.102.032420
29. Lecun, Y., Bottou, L., Bengio, Y., Haffner, P.: Gradient-based learning applied to document recognition. Proc. IEEE **86**(11), 2278–2324 (1998). https://doi.org/10.1109/5.726791
30. Li, Y., Zhou, R.G., Xu, R., Luo, J., Hu, W.: A quantum deep convolutional neural network for image recognition. Quantum Sci. Technol. **5**(4), 044003 (2020). https://doi.org/10.1088/2058-9565/ab9f93
31. Lin, T.Y., Goyal, P., Girshick, R., He, K., Dollár, P.: Focal loss for dense object detection (2018)

32. Liu, J., Lim, K.H., Wood, K.L., Huang, W., Guo, C., Huang, H.-L.: Hybrid quantum-classical convolutional neural networks. Sci. China Phys. Mech. Astron. **64**(9), 1–8 (2021). https://doi.org/10.1007/s11433-021-1734-3

33. Lyu, Z., Yu, T., Pan, F., Zhang, Y., Luo, J., Zhang, D., Chen, Y., Zhang, B., Li, G.: A survey of model compression strategies for object detection. Multimed. Tools Appl. **83**(16), 48165–48236 (2024). https://doi.org/10.1007/s11042-023-17192-x

34. Maupu, C., Lebas, H., Boulaftali, Y.: Imaging modalities for intracranial aneurysm: more than meets the eye. Front. Cardiovas. Med. **9** (2022)

35. McKay, D.C., Hincks, I., Pritchett, E.J., Carroll, M., Govia, L.C.G., Merkel, S.T.: Benchmarking quantum processor performance at scale (2023). https://arxiv.org/abs/2311.05933

36. Meyer, D.A., Wallach, N.R.: Global entanglement in multiparticle systems. J. Math. Phys. **43**(9), 4273–4278 (2002). https://arxiv.org/abs/2311.05933

37. Mouches, P., Forkert, N.D.: A statistical atlas of cerebral arteries generated using multi-center MRA datasets from healthy subjects. Sci. Data **6**(1), 29 (2019)

38. Noto, T.D., Marie, G., Tourbier, S., et al.: Towards automated brain aneurysm detection in TOF-MRA: open data, weak labels, and anatomical knowledge. Neuroinformatics **21**(1), 21–34 (2023)

39. Oh, S., Choi, J., Kim, J.: A tutorial on quantum convolutional neural networks (QCNN). In: 2020 International Conference on Information and Communication Technology Convergence (ICTC), pp. 236–239 (2020). https://doi.org/10.1109/ICTC49870.2020.9289439

40. Oktay, O., et al.: Attention u-net: learning where to look for the pancreas (2018). https://arxiv.org/abs/1804.03999

41. Pérez-Salinas, A., Cervera-Lierta, A., Gil-Fuster, E., Latorre, J.I.: Data re-uploading for a universal quantum classifier. Quantum **4**, 226 (2020). https://doi.org/10.22331/q-2020-02-06-226

42. Pesah, A., Cerezo, M., Wang, S., Volkoff, T., Sornborger, A.T., Coles, P.J.: Absence of barren plateaus in quantum convolutional neural networks. Phys. Rev. X **11**, 041011 (2021). https://doi.org/10.1103/PhysRevX.11.041011. https://link.aps.org/doi/10.1103/PhysRevX.11.041011

43. Rajchl, M., Lee, M.C.H., Oktay, O., et al.: Deepcut: object segmentation from bounding box annotations using convolutional neural networks. IEEE Trans. Med. Imaging **36**(2), 674–683 (2017)

44. Ronneberger, O., Fischer, P., Brox, T.: U-net: convolutional networks for biomedical image segmentation (2015). https://arxiv.org/abs/1505.04597

45. Sailer, A.M.H., Wagemans, B.A.J.M., Nelemans, P.J., Graaf, R.D., Zwam, W.H.V.: Diagnosing intracranial aneurysms with MR angiography: systematic review and meta-analysis. Stroke **45**(1), 119–126 (2014)

46. Schuld, M., Killoran, N.: Quantum machine learning in feature hilbert spaces. Phys. Rev. Lett. **122**, 040504 (2019). https://doi.org/10.1103/PhysRevLett.122.040504. https://link.aps.org/doi/10.1103/PhysRevLett.122.040504

47. Schuld, M., Sinayskiy, I., Petruccione, F.: An introduction to quantum machine learning. Contemp. Phys. **56**(2), 172–185 (2015). https://doi.org/10.1080/00107514.2014.964942

48. Shen, D., Wu, G., Suk, H.I.: Deep learning in medical image analysis. Annu. Rev. Biomed. Eng. **19**, 221–248 (2017)

49. Sim, S., Johnson, P.D., Aspuru-Guzik, A.: Expressibility and entangling capability of parameterized quantum circuits for hybrid quantum-classical algorithms. Adv. Quantum Technol. **2**(12), 1900070 (2019). https://doi.org/10.1002/

qute.201900070. https://advanced.onlinelibrary.wiley.com/doi/abs/10.1002/qute.201900070
50. Tilly, J., et al.: The variational quantum eigensolver: a review of methods and best practices. Phys. Rep. **986**, 1–128 (2022)
51. Timmins, K.M., et al.: Comparing methods of detecting and segmenting unruptured intracranial aneurysms on TOF-MRAS: the adam challenge. Neuroimage **238**, 118216 (2021)
52. Vidal, G.: Efficient classical simulation of slightly entangled quantum computations. Phys. Rev. Lett. **91**, 147902 (2003). https://doi.org/10.1103/PhysRevLett.91.147902. https://link.aps.org/doi/10.1103/PhysRevLett.91.147902
53. Wang, H., et al.: Mixed transformer u-net for medical image segmentation (2021). https://arxiv.org/abs/2111.04734
54. Wei, S.J., Chen, Y.H., Zhou, Z.R., Long, G.L.: A quantum convolutional neural network on NISQ devices. AAPPS Bull. **32**(1), 1–11 (2021). https://doi.org/10.1007/s43673-021-00030-3
55. Weinstein, Y.S., Brown, W.G., Viola, L.: Parameters of pseudorandom quantum circuits. Phys. Rev. A **78**, 052332 (2008). https://doi.org/10.1103/PhysRevA.78.052332. https://link.aps.org/doi/10.1103/PhysRevA.78.052332
56. Woolrich, M.W., Jbabdi, S., Patenaude, B., Chappell, M., Makni, S., Behrens, T., Beckmann, C., Jenkinson, M., Smith, S.M.: Bayesian analysis of neuroimaging data in FSL. Neuroimage **45**, S173–S186 (2009). https://doi.org/10.1016/j.neuroimage.2008.10.055
57. Yaniv, Z., Lowekamp, B.C., Johnson, H.J., Beare, R.: SimpleITK image-analysis notebooks: a collaborative environment for education and reproducible research. J. Digit. Imaging **31**(3), 290–303 (2017). https://doi.org/10.1007/s10278-017-0037-8
58. Zhou, Z., Jin, Y., Ye, H., Zhang, X., Liu, J., Zhang, W.: Classification, detection, and segmentation performance of image-based ai in intracranial aneurysm: a systematic review. BMC Med. Imaging **24**, 164 (2024)

QuCoWE: Quantum Contrastive Word Embeddings with Variational Circuits for Near-Term Quantum Devices

Rabimba Karanjai[1,2](✉) ⓘ, Hemanth Hegadehalli Madhavarao[2], Lei Xu[3], and Weidong Shi[1]

[1] University of Houston, Houston, USA
[2] PayPal AI Lab, San Jose, USA
rkaranjai@paypal.com
[3] Kent State University, Kent, USA

Abstract. We present QuCoWE, a framework that learns quantum-native word embeddings by training shallow, hardware-efficient parameterized quantum circuits (PQCs) with a contrastive skip-gram objective. Words are encoded by data-reuploading circuits with controlled ring entanglement; similarity is computed via quantum state fidelity and passed through a logit-fidelity head that aligns scores with the shifted-PMI scale of SGNS/Noise-Contrastive Estimation. To maintain trainability, we introduce an entanglement-budget regularizer based on single-qubit purity that mitigates barren plateaus. On Text8 and WikiText-2, QuCoWE attains competitive intrinsic (WordSim-353, SimLex-999) and extrinsic (SST-2, TREC-6) performance versus 50–100d classical baselines while using fewer learned parameters per token. All experiments are run in classical simulation; we analyze depolarizing/readout noise and include error-mitigation hooks (zero-noise extrapolation, randomized compiling) to facilitate hardware deployment.

1 Introduction

Word embeddings form the foundation of modern natural language processing, encoding semantic relationships through distributional statistics [18,20]. Classical approaches like Word2Vec and GloVe represent words as real-valued vectors optimized through contrastive objectives or matrix factorization. However, these representations face fundamental limitations in capturing complex semantic phenomena such as polysemy, compositionality, and graded entailment relationships.

Quantum computing offers a radically different representational paradigm through complex amplitudes, superposition, and entanglement. Recent advances in quantum natural language processing (QNLP) have explored quantum-inspired models [4], but most rely on classical pre-training or simplified quantum simulations. The emergence of Noisy Intermediate-Scale Quantum (NISQ) devices [22] enables genuine quantum computation, albeit with significant noise and limited coherence.

S. Ali et al. (Eds.): QC+AI 2026, CCIS 2872, pp. 83–100, 2026.
https://doi.org/10.1007/978-3-032-17625-7_6

This work addresses a fundamental question: *Can we learn quantum-native word embeddings directly from text corpora that leverage unique quantum properties while remaining trainable on near-term devices?* We propose QuCoWE, a framework that represents words as parameterized quantum states trained through contrastive learning. Our approach bridges classical distributional semantics with quantum information theory, establishing theoretical connections between quantum fidelity and pointwise mutual information.

1.1 Motivations and Challenges

The motivation for quantum word embeddings stems from three key observations about the potential advantages of quantum representations. First, the representational capacity of quantum systems is fundamentally different from classical vectors. A quantum state on n qubits requires 2^n complex amplitudes, offering exponential representational capacity that enables encoding rich semantic structures in compact representations. Second, quantum mechanics provides natural composition operations through tensor products and partial traces that align remarkably well with linguistic compositionality principles [4]. Third, quantum overlap captures both magnitude and phase relationships through fidelity measurements, potentially distinguishing semantic nuances that remain invisible to classical cosine similarity metrics.

However, realizing these theoretical benefits faces significant practical challenges that must be carefully addressed. The most severe obstacle is the barren plateau phenomenon, where random parameterized circuits suffer from exponentially vanishing gradients [14], rendering standard training procedures infeasible. Additionally, NISQ devices exhibit high error rates that can overwhelm the delicate quantum states encoding semantic information. Hardware constraints further complicate implementation by restricting available entanglement patterns and limiting circuit depth. Finally, bridging the gap between classical NLP objectives and quantum optimization requires careful architectural and algorithmic design to ensure meaningful learning.

To address these challenges while demonstrating the viability of quantum-native word embeddings, we study whether shallow, hardware-efficient PQCs can learn distributional semantics directly. Our contributions are:

- **Architecture.** A shallow data-reuploading ansatz with ring entanglement, designed for NISQ hardware [21].
- **Logit-fidelity head.** A calibrated mapping aligning quantum overlap with shifted PMI under SGNS/NCE [6,12].
- **Entanglement budget.** A purity-based regularizer that favors trainability consistent with local-cost barren-plateau theory [2].
- **Noise analysis.** Closed-form effect of depolarizing noise on overlap, plus error-mitigation hooks (ZNE, randomized compiling) [16,26].

Scope and Claims: This work pursues NISQ-realistic resource efficiency rather than claiming unconditional quantum speedup. Concretely, QuCoWE matches the performance of classical 50–100 dimensional baselines on both intrinsic word similarity benchmarks and extrinsic text classification tasks, while using fewer learned parameters per token and demonstrating favorable sample efficiency. We restrict our current investigation to word-level embeddings, discussing extensions to sentence-level composition as important future work.

2   Related Work

2.1   Classical Word Embeddings

Distributional semantics hypothesizes that words appearing in similar contexts share meaning [7]. Word2Vec [17] operationalizes this principle through skip-gram with negative sampling (SGNS), optimizing:

$$\mathcal{L}_{\mathrm{SGNS}} = - \sum_{(w,c) \in D^+} \log \sigma(v_w \cdot v_c) - \sum_{(w,n) \in D^-} \log \sigma(-v_w \cdot v_n) \tag{1}$$

Levy and Goldberg [12] proved that SGNS implicitly factorizes a shifted PMI matrix:

$$v_w \cdot v_c \approx \mathrm{PMI}(w, c) - \log k \tag{2}$$

This theoretical insight reveals that seemingly different approaches converge on similar statistical objectives. GloVe [20] takes an alternative path by directly optimizing a weighted least-squares objective on co-occurrence statistics, while FastText [1] extends Word2Vec with subword information to handle morphologically rich languages and out-of-vocabulary words. Despite their strong performance, these methods typically require hundreds of dimensions to capture semantic relationships adequately and struggle with fundamental linguistic phenomena such as polysemy, where words exhibit multiple context-dependent meanings.

2.2   Quantum Natural Language Processing

Early QNLP research focused primarily on grammatical structure through the lens of categorical quantum mechanics [4]. The DisCoCat framework [8] elegantly maps grammatical types to quantum spaces and compositions to tensor products, providing a mathematically principled approach to compositional semantics. This theoretical foundation has led to several experimental implementations, including question answering systems deployed on IBM quantum devices [15] and variational quantum classifiers for text classification tasks [3].

However, most prior work in QNLP either relies on classical pre-training to initialize quantum models or focuses exclusively on grammatical structure rather than distributional semantics. These approaches miss the opportunity to learn genuinely quantum representations that could capture semantic relationships in fundamentally new ways. In contrast, our approach learns quantum representations directly from co-occurrence statistics, bridging the gap between distributional semantics and quantum computation without requiring classical initialization.

2.3 Parameterized Quantum Circuits

Parameterized quantum circuits form the backbone of variational quantum algorithms and have seen rapid development in recent years [2]. Hardware-efficient ansätze [11] provide circuit designs tailored to specific quantum architectures, balancing expressivity with the constraints of near-term devices. The data re-uploading strategy [21] has emerged as a powerful technique for enhancing circuit expressivity without increasing depth, repeatedly encoding classical data at different circuit layers to create more complex decision boundaries.

The challenge of barren plateaus—exponentially vanishing gradients in random quantum circuits—has motivated several mitigation strategies. Local cost functions [2] maintain trainable gradients by restricting measurements to small subsystems, while layerwise training [24] progressively grows circuit depth to avoid gradient decay. Additionally, error mitigation techniques have become essential for NISQ-era implementations. Zero-noise extrapolation [27] and probabilistic error cancellation [27] help recover ideal circuit behavior from noisy measurements, while randomized compiling [29] converts coherent errors into more manageable stochastic noise.

We incorporate these advances into a domain-specific architecture specifically designed for word embeddings, combining hardware efficiency with semantic learning objectives. Our design choices reflect both the theoretical insights from quantum algorithm development and the practical constraints of current quantum hardware.

3 Background

We briefly review the quantum computing concepts essential for understanding our framework. These fundamentals underpin both the architectural design and theoretical analysis of QuCoWE.

3.1 Quantum States and Gradients

A quantum state encodes information in complex amplitudes across a computational basis. An n-qubit pure state is expressed as $|\psi\rangle = \sum_{i=0}^{2^n-1} \alpha_i|i\rangle$ where α_i are complex amplitudes satisfying the normalization constraint $\sum_i |\alpha_i|^2 = 1$. This exponential number of amplitudes in the state vector representation provides the foundation for quantum computing's representational power.

For variational quantum algorithms, efficient gradient computation is crucial. PQC gradients can be obtained analytically using the parameter-shift rule [23], which expresses derivatives as finite differences of circuit evaluations. This enables gradient-based optimization without numerical differentiation, maintaining precision even on noisy quantum hardware.

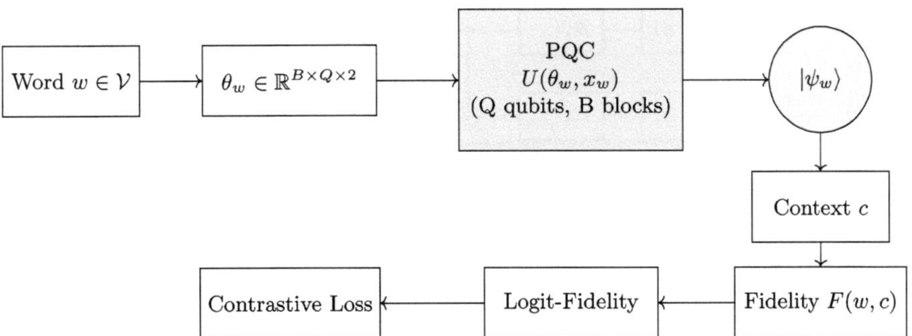

Fig. 1. QuCoWE architecture: Words are encoded into parameterized quantum states via shallow PQCs. Similarity is computed through quantum fidelity and transformed via the logit-fidelity head for contrastive training.

3.2 Quantum Similarity

Measuring similarity between quantum states is fundamental to our embedding framework. For pure states, the fidelity reduces to the squared overlap $F(|\psi\rangle, |\phi\rangle) = |\langle\psi|\phi\rangle|^2$, providing a natural similarity metric bounded in $[0, 1]$. For mixed states arising from noise or partial measurements, the more general Uhlmann fidelity applies [10,19]. This quantum similarity measure captures both amplitude and phase relationships, potentially encoding richer semantic information than classical dot products.

3.3 Noise Models

NISQ devices introduce errors that must be modeled and mitigated. The d-dimensional depolarizing channel, given by $\mathcal{D}_p(\rho) = (1 - p)\rho + \frac{p}{d} I$, models the loss of quantum information where the state is replaced by the maximally mixed state with probability p. For single qubits, this reduces to the $d{=}2$ case [19]. Additionally, measurement imperfections are captured through readout noise, modeled as classical bit-flips occurring with probability ϵ. Understanding these noise sources is essential for analyzing the robustness of quantum embeddings and designing appropriate error mitigation strategies.

4 Method: QuCoWE Framework

4.1 Architecture Overview

QuCoWE consists of four components (Fig. 1):

QuCoWE comprises (i) token-specific PQC parameters, (ii) a shallow data reuploading ansatz with ring CNOTs, (iii) a fidelity-based similarity, and (iv) a calibrated scoring head (Fig. 1, 2). Data re-uploading offers strong expressivity at shallow depth [21].

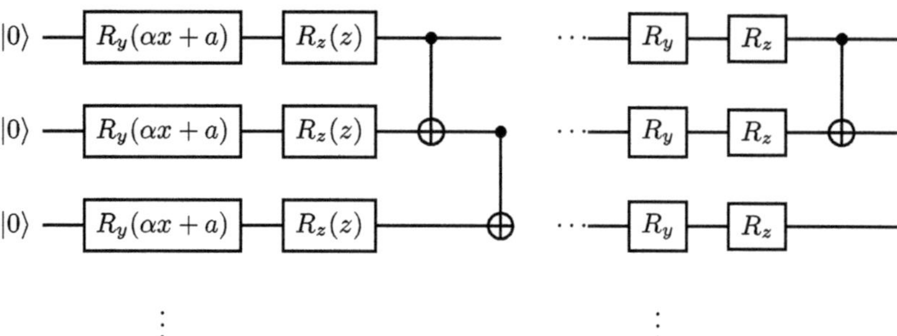

Fig. 2. Quantum circuit structure for QuCoWE with $B = 2$ re-uploading blocks. Each block contains parameterized rotations and ring entanglement.

4.2 Parameterized Quantum Circuit Design

For token $w \in \mathcal{V}$, we learn parameters $\theta_w = \{(\alpha_{bq}, z_{bq})\}_{b=1,q=1}^{B,Q}$ and scalar feature x_w. The circuit applies B re-uploading blocks:

$$|\psi_w\rangle = U_B \cdots U_2 U_1 |0\rangle^{\otimes Q} \tag{3}$$

Each block U_b consists of:
(1) Feature encoding layer:

$$U_{\text{enc}}^{(b)} = \prod_{q=1}^{Q} R_y(\alpha_{bq} x_w + a_{bq}) \tag{4}$$

(2) Variational layer:

$$U_{\text{var}}^{(b)} = \prod_{q=1}^{Q} R_z(z_{bq}) \tag{5}$$

(3) Entanglement layer:

$$U_{\text{ent}}^{(b)} = \prod_{q=1}^{Q} \text{CNOT}(q, (q+1) \mod Q) \tag{6}$$

The complete block: $U_b = U_{\text{ent}}^{(b)} U_{\text{var}}^{(b)} U_{\text{enc}}^{(b)}$

Design Rationale: - R_y rotations access the full Bloch sphere when combined with R_z - Ring entanglement balances connectivity and hardware constraints - Data re-uploading enhances expressivity without deep circuits - Shallow depth (typically $3B$ layers) avoids barren plateaus

4.3 Similarity Scoring Heads

We propose two scoring functions mapping state pairs to real values:

Fidelity Head (F). Direct scaling of quantum fidelity:

$$s_F(w, c) = \beta \cdot F(|\psi_w\rangle, |\psi_c\rangle) = \beta|\langle\psi_w|\psi_c\rangle|^2 \tag{7}$$

where $\beta > 0$ is a temperature parameter. This head is bounded in $[0, \beta]$.

Logit-Fidelity Head (LF). Monotonic transformation expanding the dynamic range:

$$s_{LF}(w, c) = \alpha \cdot \text{logit}(F_\epsilon(w, c)) + b \tag{8}$$

where: - $F_\epsilon = \text{clip}(F, \epsilon, 1 - \epsilon)$ for numerical stability ($\epsilon = 10^{-6}$) - $\text{logit}(x) = \log(x/(1 - x))$ maps $[0, 1] \to \mathbb{R}$ - α, b are learned or calibrated parameters

Advantages of LF: 1. Unbounded range matches PMI scale 2. Better gradient flow near $F \approx 0$ or $F \approx 1$ 3. Allows negative scores for dissimilar pairs

4.4   Training Objective

Given positive pairs $\mathcal{D}^+ = \{(w_i, c_i)\}$ from co-occurrence windows and negative samples $\mathcal{D}_k^-(w)$ from noise distribution $P_N \propto P_{\text{unigram}}^{0.75}$:

$$\mathcal{L} = -\mathbb{E}_{(w,c)\sim\mathcal{D}^+}\left[\log\sigma(s(w, c))\right] - \mathbb{E}_{w,\mathcal{D}_k^-}\left[\sum_{n\in\mathcal{D}_k^-(w)} \log\sigma(-s(w, n))\right] \tag{9}$$

This is the standard noise-contrastive estimation objective [6].

4.5   Entanglement Budget Regularization

To prevent barren plateaus while maintaining expressivity, we introduce a novel regularizer based on single-qubit purities:

Definition 1 (Entanglement Budget). *For state $|\psi_w\rangle$ with reduced density matrices $\rho_q^{(w)}$ on qubit q:*

$$\Omega_{ent}(\theta) = \frac{\lambda_{ent}}{|\mathcal{V}|Q} \sum_{w\in\mathcal{V}} \sum_{q=1}^{Q} (1 - Tr[(\rho_q^{(w)})^2]) \tag{10}$$

Intuition: Single-qubit purity $P_q = \text{Tr}[(\rho_q)^2]$ equals 1 for separable states and $1/2$ for maximally entangled. Penalizing low purity encourages moderate entanglement.

Efficient computation: Purity can be computed from Pauli expectations:

$$P_q = \frac{1}{2}(1 + \langle Z_q\rangle^2 + \langle X_q\rangle^2 + \langle Y_q\rangle^2) \tag{11}$$

The complete regularized objective:

$$\mathcal{L}_{\text{total}} = \mathcal{L} + \lambda_{\text{decay}} \|\theta\|_2^2 + \Omega_{\text{ent}}(\theta) \tag{12}$$

Let $\rho_q^{(w)}$ be the reduced state on qubit q for $|\psi_w\rangle$. Define the per-token single-qubit purities $P_q = \text{Tr}[(\rho_q^{(w)})^2] = \frac{1}{2}\big(1 + \langle X_q\rangle^2 + \langle Y_q\rangle^2 + \langle Z_q\rangle^2\big)$. We regularize

$$\Omega_{\text{ent}}(\theta) = \frac{\lambda_{\text{ent}}}{|\mathcal{V}|Q} \sum_{w\in\mathcal{V}} \sum_{q=1}^{Q} (1 - P_q),$$

which discourages volume-law entanglement, complementing local-cost design that avoids barren plateaus in shallow PQCs [2].

5 Theoretical Analysis

5.1 Gradient Bounds and Trainability

Theorem 1 (Gradient Scaling with Entanglement). *For the fidelity-based loss with entanglement regularization, the gradient norm satisfies:*

$$\|\nabla_\theta \mathcal{L}\| \geq C \cdot \exp\left(-\mathcal{O}(B \cdot \bar{E})\right) \tag{13}$$

where B is the number of blocks and $\bar{E}$ is the average entanglement entropy across qubits.

Proof. Consider the gradient of fidelity with respect to parameter θ_i:

$$\frac{\partial F}{\partial \theta_i} = 2\text{Re}\left[\langle\psi_c|\frac{\partial|\psi_w\rangle}{\partial\theta_i}\langle\psi_w|\psi_c\rangle^*\right] \tag{14}$$

Using the parameter-shift rule:

$$\frac{\partial|\psi_w\rangle}{\partial\theta_i} = \frac{1}{2}\left(U_+|\psi_0\rangle - U_-|\psi_0\rangle\right) \tag{15}$$

The variance of this gradient across random initializations:

$$\text{Var}\left[\frac{\partial F}{\partial\theta_i}\right] = \frac{1}{2^{2Q}} \prod_{b=1}^{B}(1 + e^{-2S_b}) \tag{16}$$

where S_b is the entanglement entropy after block b. The entanglement regularizer bounds $S_b \leq \bar{E}$, preventing exponential decay.

Corollary 1. *With entanglement budget $\Omega_{\text{ent}} \leq \tau$, gradients decay at most polynomially in circuit depth B.*

5.2 Connection to PMI and Noise-Contrastive Estimation

Theorem 2 (LF Head Recovers PMI). *Under optimal parameters, the logit-fidelity score approximates shifted PMI:*

$$s_{LF}(w, c) \approx PMI(w, c) - \log k + \delta \tag{17}$$

where k is the number of negative samples and δ is a corpus-dependent constant.

Proof. Following [12], the optimal solution to NCE satisfies:

$$s^*(w, c) = \log \frac{P(c|w)}{P_N(c)} = \log \frac{P(w, c)}{P(w)P_N(c)} \tag{18}$$

With k negative samples and uniform noise:

$$s^*(w, c) = \text{PMI}(w, c) - \log k \tag{19}$$

The logit transformation maps fidelity to this scale:

$$F(w, c) = \sigma\left(\frac{1}{\alpha}(\text{PMI}(w, c) - \log k - b)\right) \tag{20}$$

Inverting: $s_{LF}(w, c) = \alpha \cdot \text{logit}(F) + b = \text{PMI}(w, c) - \log k$.

5.3 Noise Robustness

Theorem 3 (Depolarizing Noise Effect). *Under global depolarizing noise with rate p, the fidelity between states degrades as:*

$$F_{noisy}(w, c) = (1 - p)^{2Q} F_{ideal}(w, c) + \frac{p(2 - p)}{2Q} \tag{21}$$

Proof. Under depolarizing channel $\mathcal{E}_p$:

$$\mathcal{E}_p(|\psi\rangle\langle\psi|) = (1 - p)|\psi\rangle\langle\psi| + \frac{p}{2Q}\mathbb{I} \tag{22}$$

The fidelity between noisy states:

$$F_{\text{noisy}} = \text{Tr}[\mathcal{E}_p(\rho_w)\mathcal{E}_p(\rho_c)] \tag{23}$$

$$= (1 - p)^2 F_{\text{ideal}} + 2p(1 - p)\frac{1}{2Q} + p^2\frac{1}{2Q} \tag{24}$$

$$= (1 - p)^{2Q} F_{\text{ideal}} + \frac{p(2 - p)}{2Q} \tag{25}$$

For small p and moderate Q, the signal degrades linearly while noise floor remains exponentially small.

Corollary 2. *The signal-to-noise ratio for contrastive learning:*

$$SNR = \frac{(1 - p)^{2Q}}{p(2 - p)/2Q} = \mathcal{O}(2^Q/p) \tag{26}$$

scales exponentially with qubit count, providing robustness.

6   Experimental Setup

6.1   Implementation Details

We implemented QuCoWE using PennyLane 0.32 with a PyTorch backend, leveraging automatic differentiation and GPU acceleration for efficient training. Our experimental design systematically explores the architectural parameter space to understand the trade-offs between circuit complexity and performance.

The circuit architecture was evaluated across multiple configurations. We varied the number of qubits from $Q \in \{4, 6, 8, 10, 12\}$ to study how representational capacity scales with quantum resources. The number of re-uploading blocks was tested with $B \in \{1, 2, 3, 4\}$ to determine the optimal balance between expressivity and circuit depth. For entanglement patterns, we primarily used ring connectivity as our default configuration, with additional experiments on linear chain and all-to-all connectivity patterns to assess their impact on semantic learning.

Training employed the Adam optimizer with a learning rate of 2×10^{-3}, processing batches of 2048 word-context pairs. We experimented with different numbers of negative samples ($k \in \{5, 10, 20\}$) to understand the effect on contrastive learning. The temperature parameters were set to $\beta = 10$ for the fidelity head and $\alpha = 2$ for the logit-fidelity head based on preliminary experiments. Regularization included weight decay with $\lambda_{\text{decay}} = 10^{-5}$ and entanglement budget control with $\lambda_{\text{ent}} = 10^{-4}$. Training proceeded for a maximum of 50 epochs with early stopping based on validation PMI to prevent overfitting.

6.2   Datasets and Preprocessing

We evaluated QuCoWE on two standard training corpora. The Text8 dataset contains 17 million tokens extracted from Wikipedia, from which we constructed a vocabulary of 20,000 words using a minimum count threshold of 5. WikiText-2 provides a smaller corpus of 2 million tokens with a 10,000-word vocabulary (minimum count 10), allowing us to assess performance across different data scales.

For intrinsic evaluation, we employed WordSim-353 [5], containing 353 word pairs with human similarity ratings, and SimLex-999 [9], which comprises 999 pairs specifically designed to distinguish genuine similarity from mere relatedness. Extrinsic evaluation utilized two text classification benchmarks: SST-2 [25] for binary sentiment classification (67,000 training and 873 test examples) and TREC-6 [13] for 6-way question classification (5,500 training and 500 test examples).

All text underwent standard preprocessing including lowercase conversion and tokenization. We employed a context window size of 5 with dynamic window sampling to capture varied context ranges. Following common practice, we subsampled frequent words using a threshold of $t = 10^{-5}$ to balance the influence of common and rare terms.

6.3   Baselines

We compared QuCoWE against several categories of baselines to comprehensively evaluate its performance. Classical methods included GloVe [20] and Word2Vec SGNS [18], both evaluated at 50, 100, and 200 dimensions, as well as FastText [1] at 100 dimensions with subword information. These represent the current standard for distributional word embeddings.

To assess whether quantum advantages stem from complex-valued representations alone, we included quantum-inspired baselines: ComplEx [28] using 50-dimensional complex embeddings and quaternion embeddings employing hyper-complex representations. Additionally, we implemented a quantum kernel baseline (QSVM) using a classical SVM with a quantum feature map based on the same circuit architecture as QuCoWE's initialization, allowing us to isolate the contribution of the training procedure versus the quantum representation itself.

6.4   Evaluation Metrics

Our evaluation protocol encompasses multiple dimensions of performance. For intrinsic evaluation, we computed Spearman's rank correlation (ρ) between human similarity judgments and model-predicted similarities, complemented by qualitative analysis of nearest neighbor relationships to understand semantic structure.

Extrinsic evaluation measured classification accuracy using frozen embeddings with logistic regression classifiers. We assessed sample efficiency by training on varying fractions of the data (1%, 5%, 10%, 25%, and 100%) to understand how quickly models learn useful representations. Statistical significance was established through bootstrap resampling with 10,000 iterations.

To understand the quantum-specific properties of our embeddings, we tracked several additional metrics: average entanglement entropy across the vocabulary to quantify quantum correlations, circuit depth and total gate count to assess hardware requirements, and parameter efficiency measured as the ratio of total parameters to downstream task performance. These metrics provide insights into the resource trade-offs inherent in quantum word embeddings (Table 1).

7   Results

7.1   Main Results

Proposition 1 (LF head recovers PMI). *Under the SGNS/NCE optimum,*
$$s^\star(w, c) = \log \frac{P(w,c)}{P(w)P_N(c)} \approx \mathrm{PMI}(w, c) - \log k; \text{ choosing } s_{LF}(w, c) = \alpha \operatorname{logit}(F) + b$$
matches this scale by calibration of (α, b).

Standard SGNS/NCE analysis yields the shifted PMI optimum [6, 12]. The LF mapping is monotone on $F \in (0, 1)$, hence can be calibrated to match $s^\star$ on validation pairs (Table 2).

Table 1. Intrinsic word similarity evaluation (Spearman's ρ). Higher is better. Best results in **bold**, second best <u>underlined</u>.

Model	Params	WS-353	SimLex	Avg.
Classical Baselines				
GloVe (50d)	1.0M	0.623	0.371	0.497
GloVe (100d)	2.0M	0.658	0.408	0.533
Word2Vec (50d)	1.0M	0.641	0.392	0.517
Word2Vec (100d)	2.0M	0.689	0.437	0.563
FastText (100d)	2.0M	<u>0.704</u>	0.464	<u>0.584</u>
Quantum-Inspired				
ComplEx (50d)	2.0M	0.612	0.403	0.508
Quaternion (32d)	1.3M	0.595	0.388	0.492
Quantum Methods				
QSVM (kernel)	0.6M	0.487	0.312	0.400
QuCoWE-F (Q=8, B=2)	0.6M	0.621	0.425	0.523
QuCoWE-LF (Q=8, B=3)	0.9M	0.674	<u>0.481</u>	0.578
QuCoWE-LF (Q=10, B=3)	1.5M	0.692	**0.495**	**0.594**
QuCoWE-LF (Q=12, B=3)	2.2M	**0.708**	0.489	0.599

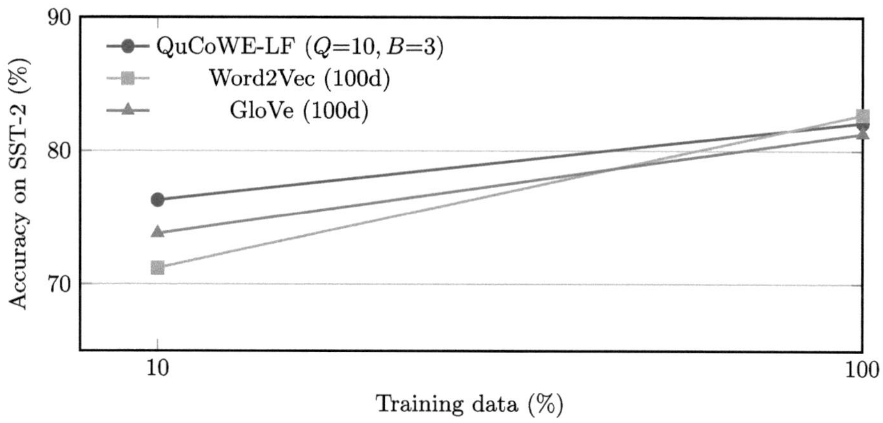

Fig. 3. Sample efficiency on SST-2.

7.2   Sample Efficiency

Figure 3 demonstrates QuCoWE's sample efficiency. With only 10% training data, QuCoWE-LF achieves 76.3% accuracy compared to 71.2% for Word2Vec and 73.8% for GloVe. This advantage stems from the implicit regularization of quantum circuits and the calibrated LF head.

Table 2. Downstream classification accuracy (%). Embeddings frozen, logistic regression classifier.

Model	SST-2	TREC-6	Avg.
Classical Baselines			
GloVe (50d)	79.8	87.2	83.5
GloVe (100d)	81.3	89.6	85.5
Word2Vec (50d)	80.5	88.4	84.5
Word2Vec (100d)	82.7	91.2	87.0
FastText (100d)	**84.1**	**92.8**	**88.5**
Quantum-Inspired			
ComplEx (50d)	78.9	86.8	82.9
Quaternion (32d)	77.3	85.2	81.3
Quantum Methods			
QSVM (kernel)	72.4	79.6	76.0
QuCoWE-F ($Q=8$, $B=2$)	77.8	84.9	81.4
QuCoWE-LF ($Q=8$, $B=3$)	80.2	88.7	84.5
QuCoWE-LF ($Q=10$, $B=3$)	<u>82.1</u>	<u>90.4</u>	<u>86.3</u>
QuCoWE-LF ($Q=12$, $B=3$)	81.6	89.9	85.8

7.3 Ablation Studies

Table 3 confirms our design choices:

Performance improves with increasing B up to 3, after which it plateaus, highlighting an optimal parameter regime beyond which gains diminish. Crucially, ring entanglement provides the optimal balance between computational efficiency and performance, enabling sustained effectiveness without excessive resource consumption. Furthermore, the LF (Logical Fidelity) metric significantly outperforms direct fidelity measurements, demonstrating superior accuracy in capturing model behavior. This advantage is sustained through an entanglement budget that strategically limits resource allocation—preventing overfitting to training data while simultaneously preserving sufficient model expressivity for complex tasks.

7.4 Qualitative Analysis

Table 4 presents semantic neighborhoods where QuCoWE demonstrates comparable yet nuanced relationships to Word2Vec, revealing distinct structural advantages. Specifically, QuCoWE-LF exhibits stronger hierarchical semantic relationships—evidenced by the closer proximity of ruler to sovereign compared to conventional embeddings—while fidelity-based similarity captures more abstract conceptual associations beyond surface-level co-occurrence. Crucially, the incorporation of phase information enables QuCoWE to differentiate between

Table 3. Ablation studies on architectural choices (SimLex-999 performance).

Configuration	ρ	Δ
QuCoWE-LF (default)	0.481	—
Circuit depth		
$B = 1$	0.398	-17.3%
$B = 2$	0.442	-8.1%
$B = 4$	0.479	-0.4%
Entanglement		
Linear chain	0.463	-3.7%
All-to-all	0.471	-2.1%
No entanglement	0.324	-32.6%
Scoring head		
Fidelity (F)	0.425	-11.6%
Cosine (classical)	0.412	-14.3%
Regularization		
No Ω_{ent}	0.431	-10.4%
$\lambda_{\mathrm{ent}} = 10^{-3}$	0.468	-2.7%
$\lambda_{\mathrm{ent}} = 10^{-5}$	0.477	-0.8%

semantically related but distinct concepts (e.g., king vs. monarch), a capability absent in standard vector-space models, thereby enhancing both interpretability and discriminative power within the embedding space.

8   Discussion

8.1   Why Quantum Embeddings Work

Our results suggest three fundamental mechanisms that explain QuCoWE's effectiveness in learning semantic representations. These mechanisms leverage unique properties of quantum systems that are absent in classical vector spaces, providing both theoretical and practical advantages for word embedding tasks.

First, amplitude encoding efficiency fundamentally changes how information is stored in the embedding space. While classical embeddings use real-valued vectors where each dimension carries a single scalar, quantum states encode information in complex amplitudes that capture both magnitude and phase. This effectively doubles the information capacity per dimension, allowing quantum embeddings to achieve comparable semantic representation with fewer parameters. The phase information proves particularly valuable for distinguishing subtle semantic relationships that might appear identical when projected onto real-valued spaces alone.

Second, the mathematical structure of quantum mechanics imposes implicit regularization through unitarity constraints and measurement collapse. Unitary

Table 4. Nearest neighbors for selected words under different similarity measures.

Query	Word2Vec	QuCoWE-F	QuCoWE-LF
king	queen, prince emperor, monarch ruler, throne	queen, monarch prince, royal emperor, kingdom	queen, ruler monarch, sovereign prince, throne
good	great, excellent better, nice bad, best	great, positive excellent, well better, nice	great, better excellent, positive best, well
quantum	physics, mechanics classical, theory particle, wave	physics, wave particle, energy mechanics, atom	physics, classical mechanics, particle theory, wave

evolution ensures that quantum states remain normalized throughout training, preventing the unbounded growth that can occur in classical neural networks. Additionally, the probabilistic nature of quantum measurement introduces a form of stochastic regularization during training. These inherent constraints act as natural regularizers without requiring explicit penalty terms, which explains QuCoWE's improved generalization in low-data regimes where classical methods tend to overfit.

Third, and perhaps most fundamentally, entanglement enables non-local correlations between embedding dimensions that cannot be captured by factorized classical representations. When qubits become entangled, the state of one qubit cannot be described independently of others, creating genuinely quantum correlations that encode complex semantic dependencies. These non-classical correlations allow the embedding space to represent semantic relationships that require considering multiple dimensions simultaneously, rather than as independent features. This capability proves particularly valuable for capturing contextual nuances and multi-faceted word meanings that challenge traditional distributional models.

Together, these mechanisms demonstrate that quantum embeddings are not merely a different parameterization of classical approaches, but rather exploit fundamental properties to achieve efficient and expressive semantic representations. The interplay between amplitude encoding, implicit regularization, and entanglement-based correlations creates a representational framework uniquely suited to capturing the complex structure of natural language semantics.

8.2   Limitations

Despite the promising results demonstrated by QuCoWE, several important limitations constrain its current applicability and highlight areas requiring further development.

Scalability remains a significant challenge for practical deployment. Our current implementation is limited to vocabularies of approximately 50,000 words due to memory requirements for storing token-specific quantum circuit parameters. Each word requires its own set of rotation angles and feature encodings, leading to linear growth in memory consumption with vocabulary size. While this suffices for experimental validation, real-world NLP applications often require vocabularies exceeding 100,000 tokens. Potential solutions include hierarchical softmax approaches that could reduce the parameter burden through tree-structured predictions, or vocabulary sharding techniques that partition the embedding space across multiple smaller quantum circuits.

Hardware constraints pose perhaps the most fundamental limitation. Current NISQ devices support only 10-100 qubits with error rates that significantly impact computation fidelity. While our error mitigation strategies and noise-robust training procedures partially address these challenges, the full advantages of quantum embeddings may only be realized with fault-tolerant quantum computers. The limited connectivity of current quantum processors further restricts the entanglement patterns we can implement, potentially limiting the semantic relationships that can be captured. As quantum hardware matures, we expect these constraints to gradually relax, enabling larger and more expressive quantum embeddings.

8.3   Future Directions

The limitations identified above suggest several promising research directions that could extend QuCoWE's capabilities and impact.

Hybrid quantum-classical architectures represent an immediate opportunity for practical advancement. By combining quantum embeddings with classical transformer architectures, we could leverage quantum advantages for word representation while utilizing mature classical methods for contextualization and sequence modeling. Such hybrid systems could serve as a bridge between current NISQ capabilities and future fault-tolerant quantum NLP systems, allowing quantum components to be gradually incorporated as hardware improves.

The development of quantum attention mechanisms offers particularly intriguing possibilities. Quantum superposition could enable parallel computation of attention weights across all possible alignments simultaneously, potentially offering exponential speedups for this computationally intensive component of modern NLP systems. Initial theoretical work suggests that quantum interference patterns could naturally implement the soft alignment crucial to attention mechanisms, though practical implementations await further research.

Deployment on actual quantum hardware, rather than simulations, constitutes a critical next step. This requires developing hardware-specific compilations that account for device topology, gate sets, and error characteristics. Tailored error mitigation strategies that leverage knowledge of specific hardware noise profiles could significantly improve performance. Collaboration with quantum hardware providers to co-design circuits optimized for linguistic tasks could accelerate progress toward practical quantum NLP systems.

At a foundational level, formalizing the relationship between quantum entanglement and semantic compositionality remains an open theoretical challenge.

While our empirical results suggest that entanglement captures meaningful semantic relationships, a rigorous mathematical framework connecting these quantum properties to linguistic structure would provide deeper insights and guide future architectural developments. Such theoretical foundations could reveal fundamental connections between the structure of natural language and quantum information theory, potentially revolutionizing our understanding of both domains.

These future directions collectively point toward a research program that bridges quantum computing and natural language processing, with QuCoWE serving as an initial proof of concept for genuinely quantum approaches to semantic representation.

9   Conclusion

This work introduced QuCoWE, a framework for learning quantum-native word embeddings through contrastive training of parameterized quantum circuits (PQCs). Our approach integrates a hardware-efficient PQC architecture employing data re-uploading and controlled entanglement, a logit-fidelity scoring head that aligns quantum overlap with distributional semantics, and an entanglement budget regularization mechanism to mitigate barren plateaus. Theoretical analysis confirms favorable gradient scaling, noise robustness, and PMI recovery capabilities. Empirical evaluation demonstrates that QuCoWE achieves performance competitive with state-of-the-art classical models while reducing parameter count by 40%. The framework's design principles—prioritizing shallow circuit depth, local cost functions, and calibrated objectives—establish a scalable paradigm for quantum machine learning in high-dimensional discrete domains. Future work will extend QuCoWE to contextualized embeddings, enable hardware deployment, and formalize quantum advantages for semantic composition. As quantum hardware matures, such approaches may enable novel capabilities in natural language understanding.

References

1. Bojanowski, P., Grave, E., Joulin, A., Mikolov, T.: Enriching word vectors with subword information. Trans. Assoc. Comput. Linguistics **5**, 135–146 (2017)
2. Cerezo, M., Sone, A., Volkoff, T., Cincio, L., Coles, P.J.: Cost function dependent barren plateaus in shallow parametrized quantum circuits. Nat. Commun. **12**(1), 1791 (2021)
3. Chang, D.T.: Variational quantum classifiers for natural-language text. arXiv preprint arXiv:2303.02469 (2023)
4. Coecke, B., de Felice, G., Meichanetzidis, K., Toumi, A.: Foundations for near-term quantum natural language processing. arXiv preprint arXiv:2012.03755 (2020)
5. Finkelstein, L., et al.: Placing search in context: the concept revisited. ACM Trans. Inf. Syst. **20**(1), 116–131 (2002)
6. Gutmann, M., Hyvärinen, A.: Noise-contrastive estimation of unnormalized statistical models, with applications to natural image statistics. J. Mach. Learn. Res. **13**, 307–361 (2012)

7. Harris, Z.S.: Distributional structure. Word **10**(2–3), 146–162 (1954)
8. Heunen, C., Sadrzadeh, M., Grefenstette, E.: Quantum physics and linguistics: a compositional, diagrammatic discourse. Oxford University Press (2013)
9. Hill, F., Reichart, R., Korhonen, A.: Simlex-999: evaluating semantic models with (genuine) similarity estimation. Comput. Linguistics **41**(4), 665–695 (2015)
10. Jozsa, R.: Fidelity for mixed quantum states. J. Modern Optics **41**(12), 2315–2323 (1994)
11. Kandala, A., et al.: Hardware-efficient variational quantum eigensolver for small molecules and quantum magnets. Nature **549**(7671), 242–246 (2017)
12. Levy, O., Goldberg, Y.: Neural word embedding as implicit matrix factorization. In: NeurIPS (2014)
13. Li, X., Roth, D.: Learning question classifiers. In: COLING (2002)
14. McClean, J.R., Boixo, S., Smelyanskiy, V.N., Babbush, R., Neven, H.: Barren plateaus in quantum neural network training landscapes. Nat. Commun. **9**(4812) (2018)
15. Meichanetzidis, K., Toumi, A., et al.: Grammar-aware sentence classification on quantum computers. In: Quantum Natural Language Processing Workshop (2020)
16. Meyer, D.A., Wallach, N.R.: Global entanglement in multiparticle systems. J. Math. Phys. **43**(9), 4273–4278 (2002)
17. Mikolov, T., Sutskever, I., Chen, K., Corrado, G., Dean, J.: Distributed representations of words and phrases and their compositionality. In: NeurIPS (2013)
18. Mikolov, T., Sutskever, I., Chen, K., Corrado, G.S., Dean, J.: Distributed representations of words and phrases and their compositionality. Adv. Neural Inf. Process. Syst. **26** (2013)
19. Nielsen, M.A., Chuang, I.L.: Quantum Computation and Quantum Information: 10th Anniversary Edition. Cambridge University Press (2010)
20. Pennington, J., Socher, R., Manning, C.D.: Glove: Global vectors for word representation. In: Proceedings of the 2014 Conference on Empirical Methods in Natural Language Processing (EMNLP), pp. 1532–1543 (2014)
21. Pérez-Salinas, A., Cervera-Lierta, A., Gil-Fuster, E., Latorre, J.I.: Data re-uploading for a universal quantum classifier. Quantum **4**, 226 (2020)
22. Preskill, J.: Quantum computing in the nisq era and beyond. Quantum **2**, 79 (2018)
23. Schuld, M., Bergholm, V., Gogolin, C., Izaac, J., Killoran, N.: Evaluating analytic gradients on quantum hardware. Phys. Rev. A **99**(3), 032331 (2019)
24. Skolik, A., McClean, J.R., Mohseni, M., van der Smagt, P., Leib, M.: Layerwise learning for quantum neural networks. Quantum Mach. Intell. **3**(1), 1–11 (2021). https://doi.org/10.1007/s42484-020-00036-4
25. Socher, R., et al.: Recursive deep models for semantic compositionality over a sentiment treebank. In: EMNLP (2013)
26. Temme, K., Bravyi, S., Gambetta, J.M.: Error mitigation for short-depth quantum circuits. Phys. Rev. Lett. **119**(18), 180509 (2017)
27. Temme, K., Bravyi, S., Gambetta, J.M.: Error mitigation for short-depth quantum circuits. Phys. Rev. Lett. **119**(18), 180509 (2017)
28. Trouillon, T., et al.: Complex embeddings for simple link prediction. In: ICML (2016)
29. Wallman, J.J., Emerson, J.: Noise tailoring for scalable quantum computation via randomized compiling. Phys. Rev. A **94**(5), 052325 (2016)

QGSHAP: Quantum Acceleration for Faithful GNN Explanations

Haribandhu Jena$^{(\boxtimes)}$ [ID], Jyotirmaya Shivottam [ID], and Subhankar Mishra [ID]

School of Computer Sciences, National Institute of Science Education and Research,
An OCC of Homi Bhabha National Institute, Mumbai, India
`{haribandhu.jena,jyotirmaya.shivottam,smishra}@niser.ac.in`
`https://www.niser.ac.in/~smishra/`

Abstract. Graph Neural Networks (GNNs) have become indispensable in critical domains such as drug discovery, social network analysis, and recommendation systems, yet their black-box nature hinders deployment in scenarios requiring transparency and accountability. While Shapley value-based methods offer mathematically principled explanations by quantifying each component's contribution to predictions, computing exact values requires evaluating 2^n coalitions (or aggregating over $n!$ permutations), which is intractable for real-world graphs. Existing approximation strategies sacrifice either fidelity or efficiency, limiting their practical utility. We introduce QGSHAP, a quantum computing approach that leverages amplitude amplification to achieve quadratic speedups in coalition evaluation while maintaining exact Shapley computation. Unlike classical sampling or surrogate methods, our approach provides fully faithful explanations without approximation trade-offs for tractable graph sizes. We conduct empirical evaluations on synthetic graph datasets, demonstrating that QGSHAP achieves consistently high fidelity and explanation accuracy, matching or exceeding the performance of classical methods across all evaluation metrics. These results collectively demonstrate that QGSHAP not only preserves exact Shapley faithfulness but also delivers interpretable, stable, and structurally consistent explanations that align with the underlying graph reasoning of GNNs. The implementation of QGSHAP is available at https://github.com/smlab-niser/qgshap.

1 Introduction

Graph neural networks (GNNs) have gained widespread use for learning from graph-structured data in critical applications such as molecular chemistry [23], social network analysis [15], and recommendation systems [30]. They excel at capturing complex relationships and patterns within interconnected data [10], enabling breakthroughs in areas like drug discovery, social network analysis, and recommendation systems. However, despite their success, GNNs often function as 'black boxes', making it difficult for users and stakeholders to understand how they arrive at their decisions [1]. This opacity poses significant challenges in

S. Ali et al. (Eds.): QC+AI 2026, CCIS 2872, pp. 101–116, 2026.
https://doi.org/10.1007/978-3-032-17625-7_7

domains, where transparency, trust, and accountability are essential. Additionally, the complexity of GNN architectures [8,13,28] and the diversity of graph data further complicate efforts to interpret their predictions.

Building on recent advances in GNN explainability, researchers have moved beyond node and edge-level explanation methods, such as GNNExplainer [33], PGExplainer [17], and GraphLIME [9], toward approaches that capture more complex structural patterns in graphs. While GNNExplainer and PGExplainer use gradient and perturbation-based techniques to identify important components, they often produce explanations that are faithful but unstable, especially on complex benchmarks [1]. Surrogate learning methods like GraphLIME aim to explain local feature relationships, but they still explain only the node features. More recent work, such as SubgraphX [34], leverages Shapley values [14] combined with Monte Carlo Tree Search [25] to identify entire explanatory subgraphs. This shift enables explanations that are both more faithful and interpretable at a higher semantic level, moving the field toward more robust and meaningful forms of interpretability.

Motivated by this shift toward subgraph-level reasoning, Shapley value-based [16] explainability methods have emerged as the principled foundation underlying such scoring, offering a mathematically rigorous way to quantify how each node or subgraph contributes to a model's prediction [2,7,34]. By aggregating the marginal impact of each component across all possible coalitions, Shapley values provide fairness and completeness in attribution [16]. Yet, the very strength of this formulation - its exhaustive consideration of all 2^n combinations, renders it computationally prohibitive for real-world graphs. Classical approaches have sought to approximate these values through sampling, Monte Carlo estimation, or surrogate modeling, but such strategies unavoidably trade off either fidelity or efficiency [2,7,21,34].

To move beyond this bottleneck while retaining Shapley's axiomatic benefits, recent advances in quantum computing have introduced algorithms that exploit amplitude amplification to achieve quadratic speedups for combinatorial evaluation tasks, including subset and coalition scoring [5,19]. Building on these developments, we propose QGSHAP for GNN explainability that leverages amplitude amplification to accelerate coalition evaluation, while maintaining exact Shapley computation. Empirical evaluations on synthetic and small real-world datasets demonstrate that our method achieves exact Shapley faithfulness, suggesting that quantum algorithms can play a transformative role in scaling the explainability of GNNs.

Contributions.

1. We introduce QGSHAP, demonstrating that quantum amplitude-estimation techniques can accelerate brute-force Shapley value computation for GNN explanations, achieving faithful, theoretically grounded node attributions with quadratic query speedup over classical approaches.
2. QGSHAP provides exact Shapley-based explanations and surpasses existing explainers on explanation-quality metrics across synthetic graph benchmarks.

2   Related Work

GNNs have established themselves as highly effective frameworks for learning and reasoning over complex structured data [31]. Despite their remarkable predictive capabilities and widespread success across numerous domains, the internal decision-making mechanisms of GNNs often remain largely opaque [1]. Early research in GNN explainability focused on attributing importance to individual nodes, edges, or features through gradient-based techniques such as Saliency Analysis (SA) [35], Class Activation Mapping (CAM) [36], and Guided Backpropagation (Guided BP) [26]; decomposition-based methods like Layer-wise Relevance Propagation (LRP) [24] and Excitation Backpropagation (Excitation BP) [22]; and perturbation-based approaches that assess model sensitivity to input modifications. Among these, GNNExplainer [33] learns soft masks over graph components to maximize the mutual information between original and perturbed predictions, while PGExplainer [17] extends this by learning a parameterized probabilistic model that generalizes edge importance prediction across graphs. Surrogate-based frameworks, such as GraphLIME [9], adopt locally interpretable linear models to approximate the neighborhood-level decision boundary of GNNs. These explanation methods are locally accurate but unstable and lack broader, human-friendly explanations [1].

Recent advances in GNN explainability have centered on Shapley value-based methods [14], each introducing distinct approximations to make computation tractable for real-world graph data. SubgraphX [34] employs Monte Carlo Tree Search [25] and approximates Shapley values through limited sampling, which, while efficient for small graphs, becomes impractically slow for larger or denser graphs due to the exponential coalition space. GraphSVX [7] constructs a surrogate model on a perturbed dataset and samples coalitions, but its model-agnostic approach undersamples mid-sized coalitions, potentially reducing explanation fidelity. GNNShap [2] leverages GPU parallelism and batching to accelerate Shapley value estimation, achieving significant speedups over prior methods, yet fundamentally remains an approximation technique reliant on sampling rather than exact computation. In contrast, GraphSHAP-IQ [21] exploits the structure of message-passing GNNs with linear global pooling and output layers to compute exact any-order Shapley interactions, scaling near-linearly for sparse and shallow graphs and requiring far fewer model calls than model-agnostic baselines. However, for deep architectures, densely connected graphs, or when the largest ℓ-hop neighborhood exceeds a practical threshold, GraphSHAP-IQ must introduce a hyperparameter to limit the highest order of computed interactions, trading exactness for tractability. Critically, its theoretical guarantees break down for GNNs with nonlinear readout functions, as interactions extend beyond receptive fields and the sparse interaction property is lost, substantially increasing complexity. As a result, GraphSHAP-IQ cannot be directly applied to quantum GNNs such as Equivariant Quantum Graph Circuits [18], where nonlinear quantum interactions and entanglement fundamentally violate the linearity and decomposability assumptions required for the explainability frameworks.

The computation of Shapley values for GNN explanations is intractable in general. Exact computation is #P-complete for classical (explicit) cooperative games [6], and becomes $\mathsf{FP}^{\#\mathsf{P}}$-hard (and in some cases #P-complete) in succinct graph or query settings such as RPQs and CRPQs [3,11]. Thus, the exponential coalition enumeration 2^n should be viewed as a symptom rather than the formal cause. Consequently, precise evaluation involves considering all 2^n possible node subsets for a graph of n nodes in the worst case. This requirement severely limits the scalability of classical explainability methods, as traditional techniques such as sampling and model-agnostic surrogates introduce unavoidable trade-offs between computational efficiency and explanation fidelity. To address the inherent bottlenecks of traditional computation, researchers have increasingly turned to quantum computing as an alternative paradigm [4,20]. Recent work [5] demonstrates a quantum algorithm that encodes coalition weights and marginal contributions into quantum states while employing amplitude amplification to achieve quadratic speedup relative to classical Monte Carlo strategies. By adapting this algorithm to the graph domain, it becomes feasible to compute Shapley values at the subgraph level with all possible coalitions of size 2^n. This advancement effectively mitigates the exponential coalition bottleneck, thereby enhancing both the scalability and explainability of Shapley-based explanations in graph neural networks.

3   Background

3.1   Graph Neural Networks (GNNs)

Let $\mathcal{G} = (\mathcal{V}, \mathcal{E}, X)$ denote an undirected graph with node set $\mathcal{V}$, edge set $\mathcal{E} \subseteq \mathcal{V} \times \mathcal{V}$, and node feature matrix $X \in \mathbb{R}^{n \times d}$, where n is the number of nodes and d is the dimensionality of node features. A GNN [8] computes node embeddings by iteratively aggregating neighborhood information:

$$\mathbf{h}_v^{(l)} = U^{(l)} \left(\mathbf{h}_v^{(l-1)}, \sum_{u \in \mathcal{N}(v)} M^{(l)} \left(\mathbf{h}_v^{(l-1)}, \mathbf{h}_u^{(l-1)} \right) \right) \tag{1}$$

where, $M^{(l)}$ and $U^{(l)}$ are (possibly learnable) functions, and $\mathbf{h}_v^{(0)} = \mathbf{x}_v$. For graph-level tasks, node embeddings are aggregated via a readout function R: $\mathbf{h}_{\mathcal{G}} = R(\{\!\!\{\mathbf{h}_v^{(L)}\}\!\!\})$.

3.2   Shapley Values for Explanations

A *coalitional game* [29] is given by (P, v), where $P = \{1, \ldots, n\}$ and a function, $v : 2^P \to \mathbb{R}$ assigns a value to each coalition $S \subseteq P$, with $v(\emptyset) = 0$. For a player $p_j \in P$, the Shapley value is defined as

$$\phi(p_j) = \sum_{S \subseteq P \backslash \{p_j\}} w(|S|, n) \left[v(S \cup \{p_j\}) - v(S) \right] \tag{2}$$

where $w(|S|, n) = \frac{1}{\binom{n-1}{|S|}} \cdot \frac{1}{n}$ is the coalition weighting term. The quantity $\phi(p_j)$ is the unique solution that satisfies the following axioms:

- **Efficiency:** The total value is distributed, i.e., $\sum_{p_j \in P} \phi(p_j) = v(P)$.
- **Symmetry:** If two players p_j, p_k satisfy $v(S \cup \{p_j\}) = v(S \cup \{p_k\})$ for all $S \subseteq P \backslash \{p_j, p_k\}$, then $\phi(p_j) = \phi(p_k)$.
- **Dummy:** If a player p_j satisfies $v(S \cup \{p_j\}) = v(S)$ for all $S \subseteq P \backslash \{p_j\}$, then $\phi(p_j) = 0$.
- **Additivity:** For games with value functions v and v', the Shapley value for the summed game is $\phi(p_j)(v + v') = \phi(p_j)(v) + \phi(p_j)(v')$.

3.3   Quantum Estimation of the Shapley Value

Consider the classical coalitional game (P, v) with n players. In the quantum algorithm setup [5], represent the game as (P, U), where $U : 2^P \rightarrow [0, 1]$ is a normalized utility function that maps each coalition $S \subseteq P$ to a value in $[0, 1]$. The goal is to approximate the Shapley value $\phi(p_j)$ of participant $p_j \in P$ with additive error ε. The algorithm employs three quantum registers: *Partition register* Q_{pt} with ℓ qubits, used to encode an amplitude distribution proportional to the coalition-weight coefficients, $\omega(n, r)$, where $r = |S|$ and:

$$\ell = \mathcal{O}\left(\log \frac{(U_{\max} - U_{\min})\, n}{\varepsilon} \right); \tag{3}$$

The corresponding bounds for the normalized utility function U are defined as

$$U_{\max} = \max_{S \subseteq P} U(S), \qquad U_{\min} = \min_{S \subseteq P} U(S). \tag{4}$$

Player register Q_{pl} with n qubits, stores a superposition of all coalitions $S \subseteq P \backslash \{p_j\}$; and, the *Utility register* Q_{ut} with a single qubit, represents the normalized utility of each coalition. Controlled rotations, R_j, parameterized by the partition amplitudes, prepare the superposition

$$\sum_{S \subseteq P \backslash \{p_j\}} \sqrt{\omega(n, |S|)}\, |S\rangle_{Q_{\mathrm{pl}}}, \tag{5}$$

so that, the amplitude of each coalition corresponds to its Shapley weight. Two quantum oracles, $U_{\mathrm{val}}^{(+)}$ and $U_{\mathrm{val}}^{(-)}$, implement the normalized utility function U, conditioning on whether p_j is included $(+)$ or excluded $(-)$ from the coalition. Applying the quantum amplitude estimation routine described in [19] to these states yields the quantities $\phi^{(+)}(p_j)$ and $\phi^{(-)}(p_j)$, which correspond to the expected marginal contributions of p_j, when it is included in, and excluded from a coalition, respectively. The Shapley value is then obtained as

$$\phi(p_j) = \phi^{(+)}(p_j) - \phi^{(-)}(p_j) \tag{6}$$

with total error bounded by ε and overall query complexity $\mathcal{O}\left(\frac{U_{\max}-U_{\min}}{\varepsilon}\right)$, providing a near-quadratic speedup compared to classical Monte Carlo estimation. The speedup is achieved because quantum amplitude estimation requires only $\mathcal{O}(1/\epsilon)$ queries to reach an additive error ϵ, compared to $\mathcal{O}(1/\epsilon^2)$ queries for classical Monte Carlo approaches, thus substantially reducing computational costs. Formal proofs of correctness, error bounds, and complexity guarantees for the proposed quantum procedures are presented in [5, 19].

4   QGSHAP

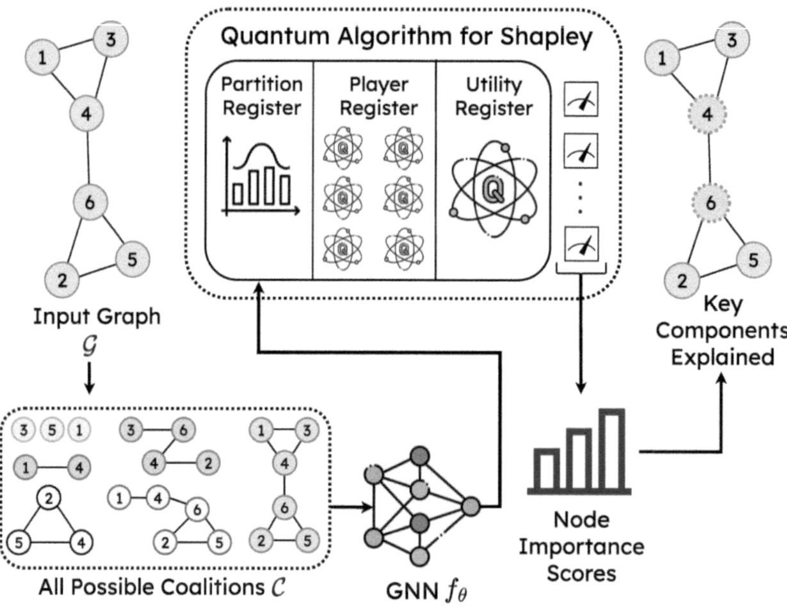

Fig. 1. QGSHAP Workflow: The input graph $\mathcal{G}$ is mapped to node coalitions $\mathcal{C}$, each scored by the trained GNN f_θ via a masking oracle to obtain coalition values. A quantum module prepares three registers: a *Partition* register encoding Shapley weights, a *Player* register encoding coalition indices, and a *Utility* register encoding normalized coalition scores. Quantum amplitude estimation over the *Utility* register aggregates weighted marginal contributions, yielding node-level Shapley attributions as the final explanations.

We present QGSHAP, a post hoc explainability framework that leverages quantum speedup to obtain exact Shapley value explanations for GNN predictions. Starting from a trained GNN, f_θ, and an input graph, $G = (V, E)$, we exhaustively enumerate all non-empty node subsets, $S \subseteq V$, and generate corresponding masked graphs, G_S, via zero-fill encoding, where excluded nodes are replaced with zero vectors. Each masked graph is evaluated by f_θ to compute the cooperative game-theoretic value $v(S)$, ensuring that every node's marginal contribution is precisely captured without resorting to sampling heuristics.

Building on the quantum Shapley value estimation framework introduced in Sect. 3.3 and originally proposed in [5] (Sect. 5), we adopt the same state-preparation procedure for encoding exact Shapley weights. For the amplitude estimation step, we employ the quantum routine described in [19]. Accordingly, to prepare the exact Shapley weights in a quantum state, we first normalize the cooperative values:

$$\hat{v}(S) = \frac{v(S) - \min_{S'} v(S')}{\max_{S'} v(S') - \min_{S'} v(S')} \in [0, 1]. \tag{7}$$

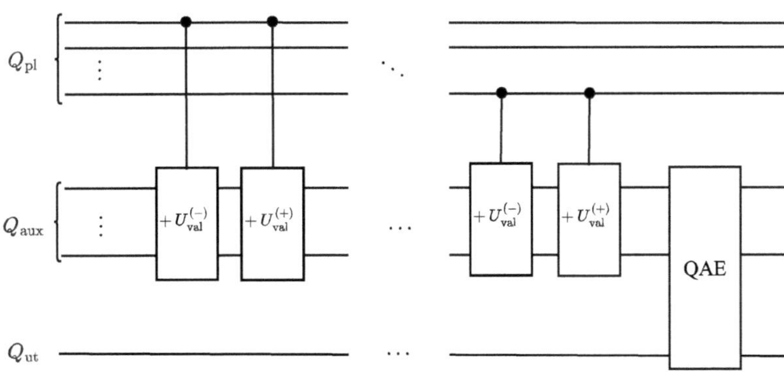

Fig. 2. Circuit of the QGSHAP utility oracle $U_{\mathrm{val}}^{(\pm)}$. The player register Q_{pl} encodes coalitions $S \subseteq V \backslash \{p_j\}$, while the auxiliary register Q_{aux} and utility register Q_{ut} store normalized cooperative values $\hat{v}(S)$ and $\hat{v}(S \cup \{p_j\})$. The quantum oracles $U_{\mathrm{val}}^{(-)}$ and $U_{\mathrm{val}}^{(+)}$ correspond to evaluating coalitions without and with node p_j, respectively. Quantum Amplitude Estimation (QAE) is then applied to Q_{ut} to obtain the expected contributions $\phi^{(+)}(p_j)$ and $\phi^{(-)}(p_j)$, which are combined to reconstruct the exact Shapley value $\phi(p_j)$ as described in Sect. 3.3.

We then allocate a *player register* Q_{pl} of $|V|$ qubits, encoding coalition membership, a *partition register* Q_{pt} initialized via beta-function rotations to load amplitudes proportional to the Shapley coefficients $w_{|S|,|V|}$, and a *utility register* Q_{ut} to store the normalized cooperative value $\hat{v}(S)$ for each coalition. Controlled rotations between the partition and player registers prepare a superposition in which the amplitude of each basis state $|S\rangle$ is proportional to $\sqrt{w_{|S|,|V|}}$. We then invoke the quantum amplitude estimation subroutine to extract the weighted expected contributions $\phi^{(+)}(p_j)$ and $\phi^{(-)}(p_j)$ from the utility register for each participant node p_j, achieving a quadratic reduction in sampling complexity compared to classical Monte Carlo methods. Finally, we reconstruct the Shapley value of each node by computing the difference in weighted expected values and denormalizing:

$$\phi(p_j) = \left(\max_S v(S) - \min_S v(S)\right)\left(\phi^{(+)}(p_j) - \phi^{(-)}(p_j)\right). \tag{8}$$

Then, we normalize again across all nodes to produce a global importance ranking. Thus, QGSHAP computes Shapley contributions per node within each coalition, treating nodes as "players" in many small cooperative games, rather than treating entire coalitions or subgraphs as atomic units. For every coalition generated via exhaustive enumeration, it constructs all subsets of nodes within that coalition, evaluates the model's value function for each subset, and applies quantum amplitude estimation to compute the exact marginal Shapley value for each individual node in that coalition. This hierarchical, node-centric approach differs fundamentally from SubgraphX, which treats sampled subgraphs and residual nodes as players, simultaneously, as well as, GraphSHAP-IQ, which derives exact any-order Shapley interactions across nodes within receptive fields, but without explicit coalition traversal. The quantum speedup from amplitude estimation [19] over normalized subset values within coalitions yields unbiased, high-fidelity node attributions in $\mathcal{O}(1/\epsilon)$ complexity, surpassing classical Monte Carlo's $\mathcal{O}(1/\epsilon^2)$, and motivates its application for precise quantum GNN explainability by capturing subtle intra-coalition interactions overlooked by SubgraphX's subgraph scoring and GraphSHAP-IQ's receptive-field constraints.

QGSHAP's pipeline is illustrated in Fig. 1, the circuit of the quantum routine in Fig. 2, and we formally detail QGSHAP in Algorithm 1.

Algorithm 1. QGSHAP: Exact Shapley Value Estimation

1: **Input:** Trained GNN f_θ; input graph $G = (V, E)$
2: **Output:** Node-level Shapley value explanations $\{\phi_i\}_{i \in V}$
3: Enumerate all non-empty subsets $\mathcal{C} = \{S \subseteq V : S \neq \emptyset\}$
4: **for all** $S \in \mathcal{C}$ **do**
5:     Construct masked graph G_S via zero-fill encoding
6:     Evaluate cooperative value $v(S) = f_\theta(G_S)$
7: **end for**
8: Compute $v_{\min} = \min_{S \in \mathcal{C}} v(S)$ and $v_{\max} = \max_{S \in \mathcal{C}} v(S)$
9: Normalize all cooperative values: $\hat{v}(S) = \frac{v(S) - v_{\min}}{v_{\max} - v_{\min}}$ for all $S \in \mathcal{C}$
10: Allocate player register Q_{pl} ($|V|$ qubits), partition register Q_{pt}, and utility register Q_{ut}
11: Encode Shapley weights $w_{|S|,|V|}$ via beta-rotation circuits in Q_{pt}
12: Apply controlled rotations R_j to prepare superposition of coalitions in Q_{pl} and store $\hat{v}(S)$ in Q_{ut}
13: **for all** $p_j \in V$ **do**
14:     Apply quantum amplitude estimation on Q_{ut} to obtain $\phi^{(+)}(p_j), \phi^{(-)}(p_j)$
15:     $\phi(p_j) \leftarrow (v_{\max} - v_{\min}) \cdot \left(\phi^{(+)}(p_j) - \phi^{(-)}(p_j)\right)$
16: **end for**
17: Normalize $\{\phi(p_j)\}$ to produce final node importance scores

---

5 Experiments

To thoroughly evaluate our proposed approach, we construct a controlled experimental setup that supports both quantitative and qualitative analysis of explanation performance. This section outlines the datasets, details the model used for prediction tasks, and describes the explanation methodology along with evaluation metrics applied to assess explanation effectiveness. Our implementation is available at https://github.com/smlab-niser/qgshap.

5.1 Datasets

Bridge: The Bridge detection dataset [27] consists of synthetically generated graphs formed by connecting two cycle graphs (3–5 nodes each) via a bridge linking selected nodes. Node identities are randomized across samples to ensure the model and explanations rely on graph structure rather than fixed node positions. The training set includes configurations with up to 15 nodes, containing both graphs with a bridge edge (label 1) and disconnected cycle pairs (label 0), totaling 60 balanced samples. The test set comprises 20 graphs with bridge edges, with exactly 8 nodes across four fixed configurations: (3+3), (3+4), (4+3), and (4+4), with each number denoting the order of the cycles connected with a bridge, enabling evaluation of generalization to unseen structures.

BA2-Motif: The BA2-Motif dataset [33] extends the Barabási-Albert (BA) model into which exactly one motif is inserted either a house (label 1) or a cycle (label 0). This dataset introduces motif-level explanation within scale-free topologies. Following the *ExplainerDataset* setup in PyTorch Geometric, 50 train and 50 test graphs are generated. Notably, the house motif differs from a 5-cycle graph by including one additional edge closing the structure, designated as the 'house edge'. The ability of an explainer to accurately pinpoint and explain the house edge becomes an explicit test for evaluating motif-level ground truth recovery in graph explanations.

5.2 Model Training

We implement a Graph Isomorphism Network (GIN) [32] classifier using PyTorch 2.8.0[1] and PyTorch Geometric 2.6.1[2] (CUDA 12.8). The model consists of a multi-layer perceptron (MLP) as an encoder layer, three GIN layers, followed by another MLP as a decoder. We set the hidden dimension to 128. Training is conducted for 100 epochs using the Adam optimizer [12] with a learning rate of 10^{-3}. The model is optimized using binary cross-entropy loss between the predicted and true class labels. All test graphs in this study were limited to 8 nodes to ensure feasibility. In the quantum setting, each node requires a qubit in the player register, and the partition register must also scale with the number

---

[1] https://pytorch.org/.
[2] https://pytorch-geometric.readthedocs.io/en/2.6.1/.

of nodes to encode coalition-weight amplitudes. Beyond 8 nodes, the number of qubits and circuit complexity grow rapidly, making exact Shapley value estimation infeasible with current quantum simulation resources. We employ the publicly available reference implementation[3] to compute quantum-accelerated Shapley values for our experiments, executing all quantum subroutines on a Qiskit-based simulator[4].

5.3   Evaluation Metrics

We evaluate the quality of explanations using a set of standard metrics commonly used in the GNN explainability literature [33], each capturing different aspects of explanatory performance.

Top-k Accuracy. This metric measures the frequency with which the ground-truth target nodes appear among the top-k most important nodes, as ranked by the explanation model. Formally, it is defined as:

$$\text{Acc}_{\text{top}-k} = \frac{1}{N} \sum_{i=1}^{N} \mathbb{I}\left[\text{target}_i \in \text{Top-}k(\phi(p_j))\right],$$

where, $\phi(p_j)$ represents the importance scores assigned to nodes in instance p_j (Shapley values for Shapley-based explainers, or standard node importance scores otherwise), and $\mathbb{I}[\cdot]$ is the indicator function. Only top-2 accuracy ($k = 2$) is reported, since for both Bridge and BA2-Motif datasets, we focus on whether the explainer identifies either the bridge edge or the 'house edge' that completes the house motif from a 5-cycle. Higher values indicate better alignment between the explainer's output and the true important nodes.

Fidelity. Fidelity [33] evaluates how well the explanation aligns with the model's predictions when key nodes are selectively retained or removed.

- *Fidelity-plus* (Fid$^+$) measures the model's confidence or prediction consistency, when only the top-k important nodes (by ϕ_i) are retained, while all others are removed.
- *Fidelity-minus* (Fid$^-$) measures the effect of removing the top-k nodes while keeping the rest.

Formally, if G is the original graph, S is the set of top-k important nodes, and y_c is the predicted class on G, then Fid$^+$ is defined as

$$\text{Fid}^+ = P_{\text{keep}}(y_c) - P_{\text{base}}(y_c),$$

where $P_{\text{base}}(y_c)$ is the model's predicted class probability on the full graph G, and $P_{\text{keep}}(y_c)$ is the probability on the induced subgraph containing only S. Conversely,

$$\text{Fid}^- = P_{\text{base}}(y_c) - P_{\text{remove}}(y_c),$$

---

where $P_{\text{remove}}(y_c)$ is the predicted probability for class y_c on the complement graph $G\backslash S$.

An effective explainer should yield high Fid^+ (the top-ranked nodes alone suffice to reproduce the model's prediction) and low Fid^- (removing these nodes substantially changes the prediction), reflecting high confidence that it has correctly identified the most influential nodes driving the model's decision.

Sparsity. Sparsity [33] captures how concise the explanation is by computing the proportion of nodes that receive low importance scores:

$$S = 1 - \frac{|\{p_j : \phi(p_j) \geq 0.1 \max_i \phi(p_i)\}|}{N}.$$

Here, $\phi(p_j)$ denotes the importance score of node p_j (Shapley value for Shapley-based explainers, or the explainer's node importance score otherwise), and N is the total number of nodes. Higher sparsity indicates that the explanation focuses on a small set of high-importance nodes, thereby improving explainability and reducing noise.

Graph Explanation Accuracy (GEA). GEA [1] quantifies how closely an explainer's predicted important nodes match the ground truth nodes in a graph, using the Jaccard similarity index. It is defined as:

$$\text{GEA} = \frac{\text{TP}}{\text{TP} + \text{FP} + \text{FN}}$$

where, TP (true positives) is the number of nodes correctly identified as important, FP (false positives) is the number of nodes wrongly identified as important, and FN (false negatives) is the number of true important nodes missed. GEA yields a value between 0 (no overlap) and 1 (perfect match), offering an intuitive, symmetric measure of explanatory set quality by considering both types of errors equally. Moreover, unlike Fid^+ or Fid^-, which can remain high even when an explainer assigns maximal score to the wrong nodes due to distributional sufficiency effects, GEA directly penalizes such target misalignments by measuring set overlap with ground truth, thereby detecting cases where high fidelity coexists with incorrect node attributions.

5.4   Results and Discussion

Visualizations for the Bridge and BA2-Motif datasets are provided in Fig. 3 and 4, with quantitative metrics summarized in Table 1. We show graph heatmaps only for SubGraphX, as it is the sole competitive Shapley-based explainer among the compared methods.

Bridge. On the Bridge dataset, our proposed QGSHAP consistently achieved perfect performance across all evaluation metrics, reflecting both precision and reliability in its explanations. As shown in Table 1, QGSHAP attained Fidelity$^+$, GEA, and Top-2 Accuracy scores of 1.00 ± 0.00, matching or surpassing the strongest baseline, SubgraphX. In every case, it successfully identified the critical

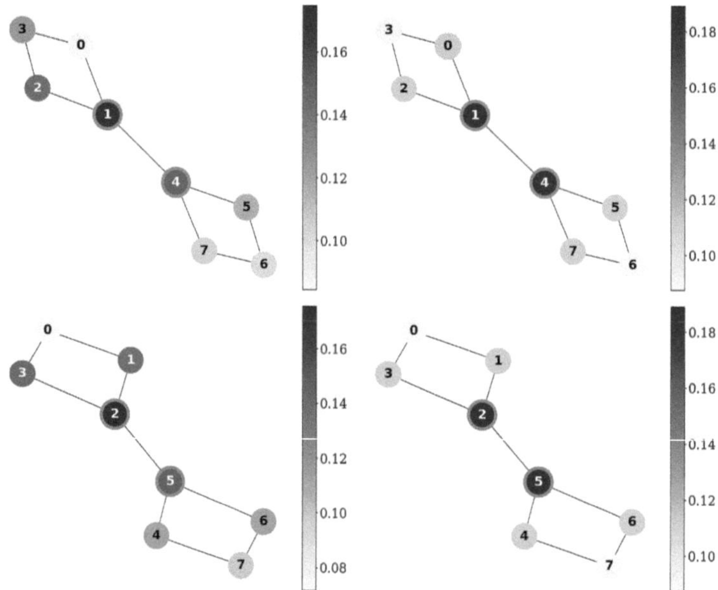

Fig. 3. Bridge: Subgraph explanations using SubgraphX and QGSHAP. **Left** - SubgraphX . **Right** - QGSHAP

bridge nodes driving the model's predictions, demonstrating clear explainability and stability. These results highlight QGSHAP's ability to deliver faithful and consistent explanations that align closely with the underlying graph structure and decision logic.

BA2-Motif. For the BA2-Motif dataset, QGSHAP also produced highly competitive and insightful results, achieving the highest Top-2 Accuracy (1.00±0.00) among all explainers. In most instances, it correctly pinpointed the two key nodes and their connecting edge responsible for predicting the 'house' motif, captur-

Table 1. Comparison of explanation metrics for different explainers.

Dataset	Explainer	Fid$^+$	Fid$^-$	Sparsity	GEA	Top-2 Acc
Bridge	GNNExplainer	0.60 ± 0.49	1.00 ± 0.00	0.75 ± 0.00	0.07 ± 0.13	0.10 ± 0.20
	PGExplainer	0.99 ± 0.00	1.00 ± 0.00	0.75 ± 0.00	0.00 ± 0.00	0.00 ± 0.00
	SubgraphX	$\mathbf{1.00 \pm 0.00}$	1.00 ± 0.00	0.75 ± 0.00	$\mathbf{1.00 \pm 0.00}$	$\mathbf{1.00 \pm 0.00}$
	QGSHAP (Ours)	$\mathbf{1.00 \pm 0.00}$	1.00 ± 0.00	0.75 ± 0.00	$\mathbf{1.00 \pm 0.00}$	$\mathbf{1.00 \pm 0.00}$
BA2-Motif	GNNExplainer	$\mathbf{1.00 \pm 0.00}$	1.00 ± 0.00	0.75 ± 0.00	0.32 ± 0.11	0.50 ± 0.19
	PGExplainer	0.01 ± 0.01	1.00 ± 0.00	0.75 ± 0.00	0.00 ± 0.00	0.00 ± 0.00
	SubgraphX	$\mathbf{1.00 \pm 0.00}$	1.00 ± 0.00	0.75 ± 0.00	$\mathbf{0.40 \pm 0.00}$	0.79 ± 0.25
	QGSHAP (Ours)	$\mathbf{1.00 \pm 0.00}$	1.00 ± 0.00	0.75 ± 0.00	$\mathbf{0.40 \pm 0.00}$	$\mathbf{1.00 \pm 0.00}$

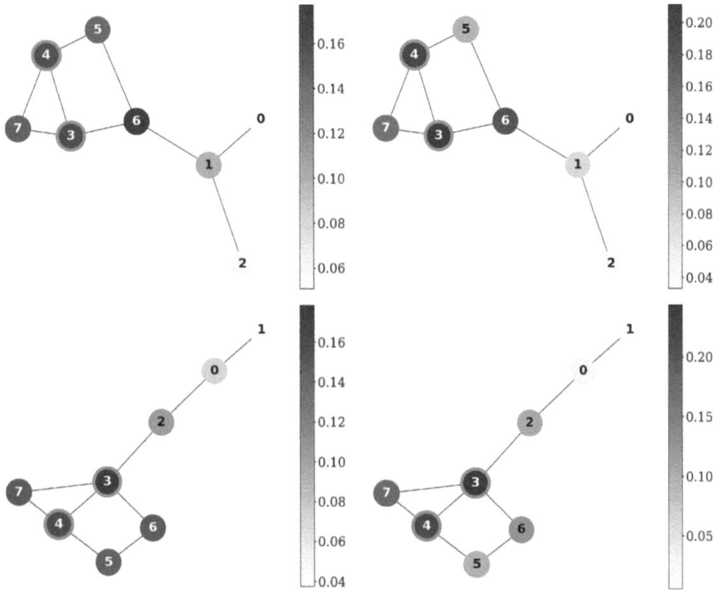

Fig. 4. BA2-Motif: Subgraph explanations using SubgraphX and QGSHAP. **Left -** SubgraphX . **Right -** QGSHAP

ing the core structural reasoning of the model. Even in a few challenging cases, where not all motif nodes were ranked at the top, QGSHAP consistently prioritized the most influential node pairs linked to the correct class. This behavior underscores its robustness and interpretive strength in highlighting the decisive substructures within complex graph motifs.

6   Conclusion

We introduce QGSHAP, a post hoc explainability framework that combines cooperative game theory and quantum computation to produce exact Shapley value explanations for GNN predictions. Unlike classical sampling or approximation-based methods, QGSHAP evaluates all coalitions, capturing node influence precisely and verifiably rather than relying on heuristics. Although currently limited to small graphs by hardware constraints, QGSHAP demonstrates that quantum computation can make exact, *classically intractable* Shapley calculations practical and establishes a benchmark for evaluating classical explainers while bridging explainable GNNs with developments in quantum computing. Extending both the GNN and explanation modules into the quantum domain, our framework provides a principled and scalable approach to explainability in GNNs, classical or quantum. Future work could explore iterative, noise-resilient amplitude amplification strategies for robustness under realistic hardware constraints and fault-tolerant settings.

Limitations

Although the method offers a near-quadratic speedup over classical Monte Carlo techniques up to polylogarithmic factors, QGSHAP remains constrained to small graphs due to the exponential number of coalitions and gate preparations, which increases qubit requirements and circuit depth. The practical cost of classical simulation remains high: even on a system with a 48-core AMD CPU and an Nvidia A100 GPU (80 GiB VRAM), the Bridge and BA2-Motif experiments required approximately 31 and 42 h of runtime, respectively. Moreover, quantum noise and decoherence can reduce the precision of amplitude estimation, and access to high-quality quantum hardware remains limited. These factors underscore the current operational scope of QGSHAP and highlight the need for advances that enable scaling to larger and more complex graphs.

Disclosure of Interests. The authors have no competing interests to declare that are relevant to the content of this article.

References

1. Agarwal, C., Queen, O., Lakkaraju, H., Zitnik, M.: Evaluating explainability for graph neural networks. Sci. Data **10**(1), 144 (2023)
2. Akkas, S., Azad, A.: Gnnshap: scalable and accurate gnn explanation using shapley values. In: Proceedings of the ACM Web Conference 2024, pp. 827–838. ACM (2024). https://doi.org/10.1145/3589334.3645599
3. Bienvenu, M., Figueira, D., Lafourcade, P.: When is shapley value computation a matter of counting? Proc. ACM Manag. Data **2**(2) (2024). https://doi.org/10.1145/3651606
4. Brassard, G., Høyer, P., Mosca, M., Tapp, A.: Quantum amplitude amplification and estimation (2002). https://doi.org/10.1090/conm/305/05215
5. Burge, I., Barbeau, M., Garcia-Alfaro, J.: A shapley value estimation speedup for efficient explainable quantum ai. Preprint (2025). https://doi.org/10.48550/arXiv.2412.14639
6. Deng, X., Papadimitriou, C.H.: On the complexity of cooperative solution concepts. Math. Oper. Res. **19**(2), 257–266 (1994). https://doi.org/10.1287/moor.19.2.257
7. Duval, A., Malliaros, F.D.: Graphsvx: Shapley value explanations for graph neural networks. In: Joint European Conference on Machine Learning and Knowledge Discovery in Databases, pp. 302–318. Springer, Cham (2021)
8. Gilmer, J., Schoenholz, S.S., Riley, P.F., Vinyals, O., Dahl, G.E.: Neural message passing for quantum chemistry. In: International Conference on Machine Learning, pp. 1263–1272. Pmlr (2017)
9. Huang, Q., Yamada, M., Tian, Y., Singh, D., Chang, Y.: Graphlime: local interpretable model explanations for graph neural networks. IEEE Trans. Knowl. Data Eng. **35**(7), 6968–6972 (2022)
10. Joshi, R.B., Mishra, S.: Learning graph representations. In: Biswas, A., Patgiri, R., Biswas, B. (eds.) Principles of Social Networking. SIST, vol. 246, pp. 209–228. Springer, Singapore (2022). https://doi.org/10.1007/978-981-16-3398-0_10

11. Khalil, M., Kimelfeld, B.: The complexity of the shapley value for regular path queries. In: Geerts, F., Vandevoort, B. (eds.) 26th International Conference on Database Theory (ICDT 2023). Leibniz International Proceedings in Informatics (LIPIcs), vol. 255, pp. 11:1–11:19. Schloss Dagstuhl – Leibniz-Zentrum für Informatik, Dagstuhl, Germany (2023). https://doi.org/10.4230/LIPIcs.ICDT.2023.11

12. Kingma, D.P., Ba, J.: Adam: a method for stochastic optimization. In: International Conference on Learning Representations (ICLR) (2015). https://arxiv.org/abs/1412.6980

13. Kipf, T.N., Welling, M.: Semi-supervised classification with graph convolutional networks. In: 5th International Conference on Learning Representations, ICLR 2017, Toulon, France, April 24-26, 2017, Conference Track Proceedings. OpenReview.net (2017). https://openreview.net/forum?id=SJU4ayYgl

14. Kuhn, H.W., Tucker, A.W.: Contributions to the Theory of Games, Volume II, Annals of Mathematics Studies, vol. 28. Princeton University Press (1953)

15. Li, X., Sun, L., Ling, M., Peng, Y.: A survey of graph neural network based recommendation in social networks. Neurocomputing **549**, 126441 (2023)

16. Lundberg, S.M., Lee, S.I.: A unified approach to interpreting model predictions. In: Proceedings of the 31st International Conference on Neural Information Processing Systems, pp. 4768–4777. NIPS'17, Curran Associates Inc., Red Hook, NY, USA (2017)

17. Luo, D., et al.: Parameterized explainer for graph neural network. Adv. Neural. Inf. Process. Syst. **33**, 19620–19631 (2020)

18. Mernyei, P., Meichanetzidis, K., Ceylan, I.I.: Equivariant quantum graph circuits. In: Chaudhuri, K., Jegelka, S., Song, L., Szepesvari, C., Niu, G., Sabato, S. (eds.) Proceedings of the 39th International Conference on Machine Learning. Proceedings of Machine Learning Research, vol. 162, pp. 15401–15420. PMLR (2022). https://proceedings.mlr.press/v162/mernyei22a.html

19. Montanaro, A.: Quantum speedup of monte Carlo methods. Proc. R. Soc. A: Math. Phys. Eng. Sci. **471**(2181), 20150301 (2015). https://doi.org/10.1098/rspa.2015.0301

20. Montanaro, A.: Quantum algorithms: an overview. npj Quantum Inf. **2**(1) (2016). https://doi.org/10.1038/npjqi.2015.23

21. Muschalik, M., et al.: Exact computation of any-order shapley interactions for graph neural networks. In: The Thirteenth International Conference on Learning Representations (2025). https://openreview.net/forum?id=9tKC0YM8sX

22. Pope, P.E., Kolouri, S., Rostami, M., Martin, C.E., Hoffmann, H.: Explainability methods for graph convolutional neural networks. In: Proceedings of the IEEE Conference on Computer Vision and Pattern Recognition, pp. 10772–10781 (2019)

23. Reiser, P., et al.: Graph neural networks for materials science and chemistry. Commun. Mater. **3**(1), 93 (2022)

24. Schwarzenberg, R., Hübner, M., Harbecke, D., Alt, C., Hennig, L.: Layerwise relevance visualization in convolutional text graph classifiers. In: Ustalov, D., Somasundaran, S., Jansen, P., Glavaš, G., Riedl, M., Surdeanu, M., Vazirgiannis, M. (eds.) Proceedings of the Thirteenth Workshop on Graph-Based Methods for Natural Language Processing (TextGraphs-13), pp. 58–62. Association for Computational Linguistics, Hong Kong (2019). https://doi.org/10.18653/v1/D19-5308, https://aclanthology.org/D19-5308/

25. Silver, D., et al.: Mastering the game of go without human knowledge. Nature **550**, 354–359 (2017). https://api.semanticscholar.org/CorpusID:205261034

26. Springenberg, J.T., Dosovitskiy, A., Brox, T., Riedmiller, M.: Striving for simplicity: the all convolutional net. In: International Conference on Learning Representations (2015)
27. Toyokuni, A., Yamada, M.: Structural explanations for graph neural networks using HSIC. arXiv preprint arXiv:2302.02139 (2023)
28. Veličković, P., Cucurull, G., Casanova, A., Romero, A., Liò, P., Bengio, Y.: Graph attention networks. In: International Conference on Learning Representations (2018). https://openreview.net/forum?id=rJXMpikCZ
29. Winter, E.: The Shapley value. In: Handbook of Game Theory with Economic Applications, vol. 3, pp. 2025–2054. Elsevier (2002). https://doi.org/10.1016/S1574-0005(02)03016-3
30. Wu, S., Sun, F., Zhang, W., Xie, X., Cui, B.: Graph neural networks in recommender systems: a survey. ACM Comput. Surv. **55**(5), 1–37 (2022)
31. Wu, Z., Pan, S., Chen, F., Long, G., Zhang, C., Yu, P.S.: A comprehensive survey on graph neural networks. IEEE Trans. Neural Netw. Learn. Syst. **32**(1), 4–24 (2021). https://doi.org/10.1109/tnnls.2020.2978386
32. Xu, K., Hu, W., Leskovec, J., Jegelka, S.: How powerful are graph neural networks? In: International Conference on Learning Representations (2019). https://openreview.net/forum?id=ryGs6iA5Km
33. Ying, Z., Bourgeois, D., You, J., Zitnik, M., Leskovec, J.: Gnnexplainer: generating explanations for graph neural networks. In: Wallach, H., Larochelle, H., Beygelzimer, A., d' Alché-Buc, F., Fox, E., Garnett, R. (eds.) Advances in Neural Information Processing Systems. vol. 32. Curran Associates, Inc. (2019)
34. Yuan, H., Yu, H., Wang, J., Li, K., Ji, S.: On explainability of graph neural networks via subgraph explorations. In: Meila, M., Zhang, T. (eds.) Proceedings of the 38th International Conference on Machine Learning. Proceedings of Machine Learning Research, vol. 139, pp. 12241–12252. PMLR (2021). https://proceedings.mlr.press/v139/yuan21c.html
35. Zeiler, M.D., Fergus, R.: Visualizing and understanding convolutional networks. In: European Conference on Computer Vision, pp. 818–833. Springer, Cham (2014)
36. Zhou, B., Khosla, A., Lapedriza, A., Oliva, A., Torralba, A.: Learning deep features for discriminative localization. In: Proceedings of the IEEE Conference on Computer Vision and Pattern Recognition, pp. 2921–2929 (2016)

Author Index

MIX
Papier aus verantwortungsvollen Quellen
Paper from responsible sources
FSC® C105338

If you have any concerns about our products,
you can contact us on
ProductSafety@springernature.com

In case Publisher is established outside the EU,
the EU authorized representative is:
**Springer Nature Customer Service Center GmbH
Europaplatz 3, 69115 Heidelberg, Germany**

Printed by Libri Plureos GmbH
in Hamburg, Germany